THE FINTECH REVOLUTION

How Technology is Redefining Money, Payments and Innovation

SAYED IMRAN QAMAR

ISBN
Paperback 979-8-89632-441-6
Hardcase 979-8-89699-361-2

Disclaimer

The facts, statistics, and information presented in this book were accurate and up-to-date at the time of writing. However, given the dynamic nature of the topics discussed, some details may have changed or been updated since then. Readers are encouraged to verify current information from reliable sources as needed.

CONTENTS

Chapter 01

INTRODUCTION TO FINTECH

1. Introduction to FinTech

In the transformative world of finance, Financial Technology—better known as FinTech—is not merely a shift but a total revolution that's been quietly rewriting the rules of financial engagement. Each swipe on your phone for a morning coffee or a swift app-based money transfer isn't just convenience; it's FinTech redefining the mundane. But, as we delve deeper into this chapter, it becomes evident that FinTech's scope stretches far beyond modernizing payments—it's recalibrating the entire spectrum of lending, investing, and beyond. Why does this matter? FinTech is not simply a trendy term - it underpins the fast-changing digital finance sector. We will explore the major changes that have driven FinTech to become a leader in financial innovation, from its beginnings to its current dominant position. We will analyze the technical language, highlight important creators, and address the obstacles present in this growing industry.

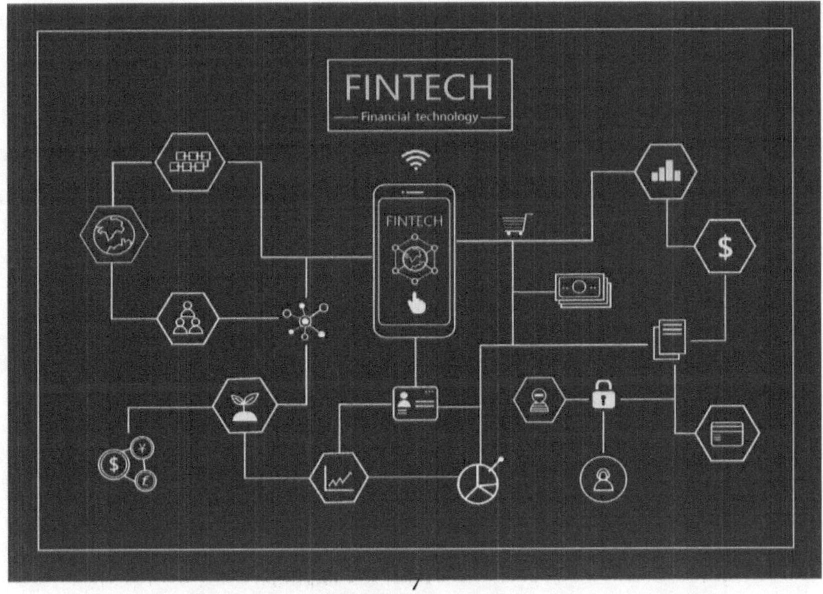

1.1 How Is FinTech Defined Today?

At its core, FinTech uses cutting-edge technology to streamline and refine both traditional and novel financial practices. The revolution isn't in the tools themselves but in the enhancement of processes. Mobile payments, for instance, existed before FinTech, but FinTech has perfected them to be simpler, safer, and more universally accessible. This sector isn't just sprouting new gadgets; it's enhancing the efficacy of financial operations, ensuring that every technological advancement bolsters security, efficiency, and accessibility.

1.2 Significance of FinTech Today

You probably use FinTech every day. Swipe a phone a few times, and you might send someone money, ask for a loan, or buy stock from a company. A decade ago, such ease would have been unthinkable. For many companies, FinTech means outsourcing functions such as automated billing, online lending platforms and fraud detection. This kind of financial services outsourcing makes everyday financial management less burdensome and could help unlock a new phase of growth for a company. However, FinTech does more than just bring convenience. It is also changing the rules about who can access financial products. There are still many people who cannot open accounts or get loans due to strict bank requirements. FinTech companies instead use technology to reach more people in more locations on a bigger scale. This includes people who might otherwise be cut off from the financial system.

In the next sections, we will explore how FinTech has grown and some of the important changes that have shaped its development. Having a sense of the past will give us a better sense of why it is such a forceful current in our contemporary lives.

1.3   The History of FinTech

To understand where we are with FinTech today, it is useful to start by looking at how it emerged, underwent different iterations and reached several milestones during its development, which made financial services more accessible, faster, and secure. Each step built upon the other in shaping the digital finance sector that we are part of. This section demonstrates that the FinTech sector was developed based on the use of technology to address the major financial challenges.

Fun Fact:

The term "FinTech" was introduced in the early 1990s, but the concept dates back to the 19th century! The telegraph, invented in 1838, was one of the first technologies used to transfer financial information over long distances, laying the groundwork for modern financial technology. FinTech may seem like a 21st-century phenomenon, but its roots run surprisingly deep!

1.3.1   Early Developments Like Credit Cards, ATMs, Electronic Banking

The first phase of FinTech evolution involved a few key innovations in the early going. In the 1950s came the credit card. If you wanted to buy something, up until that point, you would typically carry around cash on your person – which was risky. Sure, there were checks, but they weren't very reliable, and lots of places wouldn't accept them. The Diner's Club card led the way in the introduction of credit cards in the 1950s. Credit cards displayed a novel solution to allowing people to buy things without the need for money. As a result, the accessibility that credit cards brought to shopping led them to banks, and they became widely accepted at various outlets around the world. Their proposal for an 'upfront buying and pay-later settlement' paved the way for advanced payment solutions.

The first ATMs. were seen in the 1960s and '70s. Prior to the introduction of ATMs, the only way to handle one's account was to visit the branch during designated bank hours to make deposits, withdrawals and inquiries. With an ATM came a simple card and the need to push a couple of buttons, and people suddenly found it a lot easier to perform these banking activities without going to their bank at all. The emergence of ATMs. illustrates how technological advances can help make banking services available to people and, in this particular case, make it more flexible by reducing the need to conduct banking activities face-to-face in a bank. This process was often a long and frustrating process. The arrival of electronic banking in the 1980s made this process easier by enabling users to manage their accounts using a phone or a computer. This sounds quite simple compared to today's standards, but this early process of electronic banking laid the foundation for managing financial services digitally. It set the basis for the modern and quite handy digital banking tools that are available now.

1.3.2   Important Advancements in FinTech

These early advancements laid the groundwork for subsequent events. FinTech innovation accelerated from the 1980s onwards. Every decade, another breakthrough was brought to market that radically transformed financial services to the benefit of players and customers.

1.3.2.1   *The Growth in Electronic Trading in the 1980s and 1990s*

Electronic trading systems, designed to facilitate the rapid-fire buying and selling of stocks and other financial instruments, shook up traditional methods of trading. Historic means of conducting stock transactions took place largely in person, on clamorous trading floors or over the telephone with brokers. It was a method of trade that was restrictive and accessible only to those who could afford it or possessed the appropriate equipment. Electronic trading on computer networks changed all that. Instant trades became fast transactions, efficient and available, allowing even the most amateur investor to enter the stock market for the first time via online trading systems. This opened up the possibilities of investing for all of us and paved the way for further potential to manage our global finances.

1.3.2.2   The Evolution of Internet and Online Payments During the 2000s

The internet influenced the world in the 2000s. This had an impact on transactions. In the beginning, a lot of people were anxious about the idea of shopping on the Internet. They worried about their safety as well as about the safety of their financial details. FinTech companies acknowledged the difficulties and proposed some solutions that helped to develop secure digital payment solutions. For instance, PayPal, a pioneer in the field, allowed people to purchase and enjoy services without needing to enter their credit card details. Instead, they could simply enter an email address. This added an extra layer of protection for the customer. This was a great step that helped users feel safe and increased the rate at which people started buying things online. Meanwhile, online bank services started to expand. If people needed to pay bills or transfer money, they used to go to banks, but in the present day, every single transaction can be done online, providing people with an opportunity to organize and manage their money in a functional way. Another significant point is that FinTechs like PayPal and Venmo became available to the public and could be used to transfer money between each other as a peer-to-peer transaction.

1.3.2.3   How the 2008 Financial Crisis Contributed to the Advancement of FinTech Innovations

The global economy experienced a major setback with the economic crisis in 2008. People lost their confidence in traditional banks due to this crisis. A large number of banks collapsed or needed a governmental bailout in order to survive. This led to consumers and corporates looking for alternative options. The birth of new FinTech startups took place, and they offered services that were easier to understand, more accessible and simpler to use. Digital banks offer banking services without the need to locate offices. By using user-friendly apps, it is easy to access online accounts, quick loans and investment opportunities. In this period, peer-to-peer (P2P) lending platforms also emerged. People were able to send money to one another using a system without the need for traditional financial institutions. These platforms offered loans to people and small companies that were unable to get help from a regular bank before.

Coincidentally, at this point, blockchain began to attract a little attention as well. It had the capacity to enhance the security and transparency of transactions in a fundamentally new way. It heralded the arrival, at least in principle, of decentralized finance, in which assets could be traded without involving banks or other centralized third parties, a precursor to the current phenomenon of cryptocurrency, which we will talk about later on.

1.3.2.4 *Boom in Mobile Banking, Digital Wallets, and Cryptocurrencies in the 2010s*

Mobile banking grew in popularity during the 2010s because so many more people adopted smartphones. Prior to this, people could only bank from their computers or from ATMs. Mobile banking applications allow people to manage money on the go. Because of the simplicity of being able to just touch the screen, it was much easier to perform all your money management duties, such as checking balances, paying bills and transferring money. This boost in the ability to bank also helped people in less fortunate areas who may not have had many other options than local banks. At the same time, it was becoming easier to bank online, digital wallets such as Apple Pay, Google Wallet and Samsung Pay also became a new option for paying for goods. Now, people did not need to bring around any physical cash or card, and they could just tap the phone to make payments. This innovation demonstrated just how easily people could use technology in their everyday lives.

The rise of cryptocurrencies, such as Bitcoin, was also prominent as part of the changes in the 2010s. While cryptocurrencies are a newer and often overhyped idea, they represent a different way of holding and exchanging value in a society without currency. They presented the notion of decentralized finance (DeFi), which gave the foundations for financial transactions to happen without the need for 'banks.' This introduced thoughts about the future of money, with cryptocurrencies potentially replacing traditional money entirely. Later on, we will look at the key terms and ideas within FinTech that emerged from these earlier changes. Understanding these terms can help us understand more about how FinTech continues to shape the financial world.

1.4 Important Terminologies and Definitions in FinTech

Let's examine key phrases and concepts in the FinTech sector that have emerged from previous changes. Understanding these terms will allow us to witness the continuous influence of FinTech on the financial industry.

1.4.1 Blockchain

Blockchain is basically an electronic ledger. Imagine a notebook where every page records some transactions. A blockchain works almost identically, except that every time a transaction occurs, it is recorded on a 'block' in the 'chain' – in the order in which it occurred. Once something is inscribed on a blockchain, it can't be changed. That distinguishes it from a standard ledger. So, what would make this a highly secure system? One reason is the way that data is stored: not on one central computer, which could be attacked or hacked, but on many computers around the world. That makes it virtually impossible to find all the copies with the record you wanted to change. More importantly, blockchain is the technology behind various digital currencies for tracking product shipments in supply chains, for storing legal agreements, or for whatever else.

> **Fun Fact:**
>
> *Did you know that the concept of blockchain was first proposed in a completely different field? The idea of a "chain of blocks" was actually introduced in 1991 by researchers Stuart Haber and W. Scott Stornetta to prevent tampering with document timestamps. It wasn't until 2008, with the release of Bitcoin's whitepaper by the mysterious Satoshi Nakamoto, that blockchain found its revolutionary use in digital currency. Today, blockchain technology is used not only in finance but also in fields like supply chain management, healthcare, and even voting systems!*

1.4.2 Cryptocurrencies

Cryptocurrencies are a type of currency that is held only electronically, and the ownership and value of which are 'tracked' through a blockchain. The big difference between these currencies and a system like the dollars or euros used in the US or the UK is that neither governments nor banks 'issue' or 'regulate' cryptocurrencies – they are part of a distributed ledger-based network of record-keeping that sidesteps the need for a third party when users want to engage with each other. Bitcoin is the best-known digital currency, but others, including Ethereum and Litecoin, are available. People use them to buy goods and services and to make transactions in the hope that their value will increase. Cryptocurrencies are extremely volatile, and the high risk involved means that anyone thinking of investing in them should have a very promising forecast for a high return. But this potential for a novel form of means of storing and sending worth has sparked global interest and discourse.

1.4.3   InsurTech

InsurTech means 'insurance technology', using digital tools to improve insurance and make it easier and more convenient. Traditional insurance can be complex. It can require a lot of paperwork and can be slow. InsurTech businesses are changing this by providing services online or on a mobile application. For example, some InsurTech firms help people get insurance in minutes from their homes simply by filling out a form on their computers. The firms might use people's information in new ways to craft personalized policies, such as pricing car insurance based on each driver's record of driving skills. InsurTech is making insurance easier so that people can get more personalized and accessible insurance.

1.4.4   RegTech

RegTech refers to 'regulatory technology', or using technology to help businesses comply with laws and rules of the financial sector (or 'regulations'). Banks and other firms in the financial sector, in particular, must adhere to a multitude of rules to protect customers from fraud. RegTech tools are used to help firms meet this process. For example, they would look for suspicious activity in transactions and potentially spot money laundering or fraud. RegTech would help companies manage their data appropriately for issues such as privacy. In this way, firms would use technology to handle parts of this process and leave more time for them to focus on their core services while still ensuring their compliance with regulations.

1.4.5 Robo-Advisors

Robo-advisors are online programs that offer financial advice and manage investments using algorithms. Traditionally, when an individual invests, they might consult an investment advisor who can provide guidance on potential investments. A robo-advisor, on the other hand, attempts to provide many of the same services but using an algorithm over the internet. A user of a robo-advisor might complete a questionnaire that covers the person's interest and goals for investment, their tolerance of risks, and their preferred investments. The robo-advisor might recommend the selection of investments to include in a portfolio derived from the data produced by the questionnaire. This could provide wider access to investing because it is usually cheaper than hiring a financial planner and can be completed online.

1.4.6 Open Banking

Open banking allows different kinds of financial services to link up and share data securely. In the past, when we had a bank account, our bank held onto all of their customers' information privately. In an open banking system, if the customer wants to, they can give their banking information to other financial service providers. For example, a financial app that links to your bank account could be used to see where your money is going. The app could recommend where you can save money by not spending as much. Open banking makes it easier to manage your money because different financial services can link up and help you have an easier time looking after your money. However, it is important that any system putting this information together has strong security to prevent people from looking at people's personal information without permission from the customers.

1.4.7 Usage of AI and ML (Artificial Intelligence and Machine Learning) in the Finance Sector

There are different technologies used in the financial industry: AI and ML are the two most important ones that help computers learn from data and make choices. Artificial Intelligence (AI) – AI is a tool that helps computers make choices based on data sets, and it can help all different industries, including banking and finances. For example, AI can be used as a chatbot on a bank's website to answer customer questions, such as account issues, the same way a human would. Machine Learning (ML) – Machine learning refers to the ability of an AI to become better by learning from its experiences. It is frequently used for identifying deception, can analyze huge amounts of data from transactions, and can find anomalies faster than a human to prevent fraud. It can also be used for investments because it is good for studying the patterns of markets and helping with the choice of investments. These tools are fast, and they can provide data that can help in decision-making.

1.4.8   Decentralized Finance (DeFi)

Decentralized Finance, sometimes referred to as DeFi, is a system of financial services that uses blockchain technology rather than banks or other financial intermediaries. In conventional banking, the bank acts as a middleman for things such as loans, deposits and investments. For example, if you want to borrow some money, you should approach your bank for the service. DeFi allows you to interact directly instead of using the bank – this is done through digital platforms built using blockchain technology. For example, you could use a DeFi platform to lend your digital assets to someone else and earn a profit. Smart contracts are used for these platforms – these are agreements that are self-executing after the terms of the contract have been encoded into the code. This is a very efficient way of doing financial transactions because it does not require a central authority.

This means that the costs are usually lower, and the services tend to be more accessible as well. However, due to the fact that it's currently an emerging area, DeFi comes with the risk of hacking or the loss of assets if you are not careful. Having discussed these key terms, we will be able to comprehend how various aspects of FinTech are interconnected. In the upcoming discussion, we will examine the FinTech community, focusing on major participants and their impact on the sector.

1.5 The FinTech Ecosystem

The FinTech ecosystem consists of diverse participants. Each participant plays a specific role, and to fully comprehend FinTech change, it is important to understand the players. This section will explore the identities of these players, the role they play in FinTech expansion and the key FinTech hotspots.

1.5.1 Main Players in FinTech – Startups, Established Companies, Tech Providers, and Regulators

There are a few prominent players within the FinTech landscape. The first group is startups. The new companies generally focus on a certain financial problem or service, such as mobile payment, credit, or insurance. Startups are renowned for being innovative and constantly willing to try out new ideas. Because they are small and flexible, they can quickly design solutions and launch them into the market. There are also other familiar structures, such as banks and insurance firms. These firms have grown to dominate the banking sector over decades and gained much experience and respect.

Technology providers are another important part of the ecosystem. Such firms deliver the tools and technologies required for FinTech products to function. For example, they may provide secure payment gateways, a cloud platform or banks' web software. Tech providers help startups and businesses to become more efficient with the use of these tools. And there are, of course, the regulators. These are the institutions that decide the norms around how financial services should be offered. They are also responsible for ensuring that FinTech businesses meet the rules that protect consumers and keep the financial system in check. Authorities often partner with FinTech companies to ensure the proper use of new technologies.

Each of them contributes in different ways to the development of the FinTech sector: startups bring ideas, incumbents bring experience, technology providers bring tools, and regulators bring an enabling and guiding hand.

1.5.2 How Venture Capital and Accelerators Fuel Growth

Venture capitalists (VCs) and accelerators (incubators) play key roles in funding new ideas to grow. Venture capital firms provide funds to companies they believe have a chance at success. The firm will usually get a share of the company in return. The new company can use the funds to build their products, hire employees, and expand their business. Companies such as PayPal and Square were backed by venture capital in their early years. Accelerators have a slightly different function. These programs support young startups by providing funding with training, advice, and resources. For example, an accelerator for FinTech companies might run a training course for a few months, where startup companies will learn how to build their business, meet possible investors, and get feedback about their products. Accelerators can help a startup gain the needed edge and introduce them to the right people.

Venture capital and accelerators are the main contributors to the growth of the ecosystem. They provide both funds and the training needed for start-ups to turn their ideas into reality and expand their business.

1.5.3 Silicon Valley, London, Singapore – The Global Hubs for FinTech

While FinTech companies might be located worldwide, some centers have been built up as main hubs of FinTech innovation. These hubs put together new businesses, already-existing companies, financiers and technology providers, creating a network that enables the development. For some, the place where tech companies were born is Silicon Valley in the United States. It's home to the biggest tech companies, and the tech ecosystem of investors and talent is amazing. This setting is ideal for FinTech startups to thrive. The area is famous for promoting creativity and offering ample financial support for fresh concepts.

London is another hub, especially for FinTech companies in the area of banking and finance. The city is a major international hub for finance and home to many major banks and financial institutions. The regulatory environment is supportive of FinTech companies that are trying out new products. The large pool of financial knowledge and tech know-how make it the perfect environment for FinTech success. Singapore is a major hub of financial technology in Asia. The Singapore government has encouraged the advancement of FinTech by implementing proactive financial regulations and offering support programs for FinTech startups. The city is home to a number of startups and established financial institutions. Singapore is regarded as a central hub for FinTech in Asia. With its location in Asia, it can provide services to a range of very advanced markets and emerging markets.

They act as incubators for FinTech ideas, thanks to networks of investors, talent and regulation that have endowed them with substantial competitive advantages. However, other cities globally are also jostling for space as FinTech ideas spread around the world. In the next section, we highlight some of the difficulties that FinTech companies encounter as they grow and evolve within this complex ecosystem.

1.6 Obstacles Faced by FinTech

Despite these benefits, FinTech also poses some unique challenges. As FinTech grows and evolves, it has encountered barriers that can potentially either slow down its development or prevent it from reaching its full potential. These barriers are also important to understand because a company's ability to overcome them has an impact on the way it operates. This section will discuss three primary barriers: cybersecurity risks, regulatory barriers, and consumer trust and privacy concerns.

1.6.1 Potential Cybersecurity Dangers

Cybersecurity is the biggest concern in FinTech companies as FinTech platforms are a huge target for hackers. FinTech companies mainly use digital platforms to store sensitive information for online or digital payments. Since security is a big concern, these hackers will try to hack into the accounts and either steal the credit card numbers or the bank account information. Digital wallets and services for online banking store sensitive information like your password or credit card numbers so that you can use them to pay or transfer money to whoever you want. If these data are not stored properly in the system, hackers will access them and use them for their gain. To avoid this, FinTech companies will have high-security measures to protect themselves from thieves, like encryption. Encryption changes the data into code that only verified users can decode. For high-security purposes, there is also 2FA (two-factor authentication), which means a user will be required to submit two different types of information to log into their account, for example, their password and the code of their phone.

Nonetheless, those measures can be overcome by cyberattacks, and companies that embrace FinTech should constantly adjust their cybersecurity systems to ensure that their measures keep one step ahead of the new threats. The second big challenge FinTech faces is to control this war between security and cybercrime.

1.6.2   Regulatory Challenges and Compliances

Operating in such a well-regulated environment is one more challenge. Financial services are heavily regulated to make sure that they are offered on a level playing field in a way that is fair to customers, safe and transparent. This can be the case, for example, with anti-money laundering and know-your-customer rules that require suppliers of financial services to check the identity of their customers and monitor their transactions to spot suspicious behavior. Although these rules are essential for protecting consumers and the wider financial system, they can be burdensome and costly for FinTech companies to comply with. Imagine a startup offering online loans. It must make sure it is respecting all these rules in the countries in which it operates. This means it must spend time and money getting legal advice, hiring compliance staff and developing technology to comply with all those obligations.

But rules are always changing as well, making matters even more complex. When new technologies emerge, regulators have to put in place new regulations to manage the accompanying risks. FinTech firms need to keep track of these changes so as not to end up incurring fines or other penalties. Though some regulations promote innovation, too much stiffness in others can hinder it. FinTech firms must tread the fine line between innovation and regulation.

1.6.3 Consumer Trust and Data Privacy

Trust is of paramount importance in FinTech companies because they work with enormous personal and financial data (in fact, they would not survive without customer trust). FinTech services can only thrive if customers feel their information is safe and their privacy is respected. If customers believe a FinTech company is too unsafe, they will not use its services. Worries about privacy have increased now that more digital services are collecting larger amounts of data. Many FinTech apps must ask permission to access information such as contact lists, locations and transaction histories in order to provide services specifically tailored to their users. While this data can improve the user experience, worries about it being used and stored often arise.

To earn that trust, FinTech firms should be transparent about the data they collect and how it's used, should store data securely so as to prevent unauthorized access, and should allow customers to exercise control over their own data, including what information they do or don't wish to share. Consumers will have a hard time trusting FinTech companies who lobby governments to exempt them from liability after it's been discovered that they've had a data breach or have otherwise mishandled people's information. For FinTech firms, there is a need to constantly improve privacy policies and communicate clearly with customers about data protection services.

Final Thoughts

Payments are the most obvious application of FinTech, which radically transforms the process of interacting with money. Instead of swiping a card or tapping a phone into a machine, digital payments are now the lifeblood of finance. How did payment systems evolve in the past? Who is driving the change today? And what does FinTech mean for our own money? In the next chapter, we will explore the major trends and players in the payments revolution.

Digital Payments & Wallets

2.1 Advancement and Evolution of Digital Payments

In the last 30 years, the process of digital payment disruption has changed the way money moves among individuals and businesses, creating what could only be referred to as 'the new finance.' Payments were reinvented and profoundly transformed. Soon, they will permanently integrate into our day-to-day lives, from forerunners like credit cards, POS (point-of-sale) and online banking systems to contactless payments and mobile wallets. Driven by a constantly growing demand, fuelled by the thirst for more speed, ease and security in financial transactions, the development of digital payments has been nothing but a fast-paced race. If tech disruption keeps its intense pace, then in a few years, we will only see money as a letter in the space of a word that used to mean cash. In this study, we delve into the key highlights of the ongoing evolution of digital payments and the trends that are making it pick up pace on a global scale.

2.1.1   Cash to Digital Payments – The Shift

It's not just a technological transition from cash to digital money but a revolution in the relationship between humans and money. Cash was once the universal currency – cheap, physical, yet constrained. It came as physical notes pinned to wallets, counters and safes. But with digital payments, finance is more nimble, frictionless and almost immediate. Everything that once meant standing in a queue at the bank or adding up paper bills now comes down to the easy flick of a finger across a smartphone display. This change was not by chance. This is what digital payments are all about: convenience. Consumers don't have to carry wallets full of coins or worry about the safety of cash. For digital wallets, it only takes one tap or scan to complete the transaction, and it's invisibly effective. This revolution was early, but it has developed into an immense worldwide phenomenon.

From QR codes to NFC, cashless commerce has changed normal everyday transactions. It's, more importantly, changed the way we think about security — encryption, two-factor authentication and secure servers have become the invisible sword that surrounds every purchase. Digital money doesn't just substitute for paper; it enhances the efficacy and stability of our entire financial ecosystem, all without the physical limits of paper. In this progression, it is no surprise that cash is disappearing as digital money takes over.

Payments are turning the world into a cashless environment, where each exchange is a simple flow between nations, apps and networks. It's not just about ease of use but a re-evolution in trust, speed and accessibility when it comes to financial transactions.

2.1.2 PayPal's Contribution to Amazon's Growth, The Impact of Apple Pay

In the early days of e-commerce, consumer protection was crucial to the success of platforms such as Amazon, which offered a limitless number of products on the same stage but operated within a closed world of online transactions. If this were to work, consumers would need an alternative to online cash payments (where they could be easily robbed) as well as the assurance that the online bank would be as secure as the offline one while still offering all the benefits of convenience that the internet promised. It was PayPal that filled this role – and Amazon's close association with PayPal played a significant role in developing the level of consumer trust that the platform needed to succeed, just when people weren't yet accustomed to the convenience of online shopping. If Amazon was going to attract millions of users from around the world to shop on its platform, it had to work with a payment platform capable of offering cross-border transactions on a massive scale.

That PayPal achieved it with a few clicks – 'link' a credit card or bank account and payments were made – is spectacular only in retrospect. In fact, it involved a complex arrangement of cutting-edge technologies designed to be invisible to end users but allowed them to transact vast volumes across interconnected computers while protecting credit card numbers and other sensitive financial information. However, the greatest value of PayPal was not merely facilitation but also reassurance – reassuring people that it was safe to buy things on Amazon. The introduction of PayPal resolved Amazon's 'last mile' problem; it became the trusted third party guaranteeing the online exchange of money and goods between Amazon and its customers. At some level, the PayPal experience anticipated the new global connections that have become the normal way of shopping online.

On the other side of the evolution of digital payment was Apple Pay. When Apple first introduced its smartphone-powered payment system in 2014, it appeared to be pushing banks aside yet again. But Apple Pay was more than just a new way to pay: it was the future of digital wallets, fusing cutting-edge biometric technology with money. Apple Pay was fast; you just tapped your phone. But the innovation was even more transformative because it made in-person payments feel as natural and private as unlocking your phone.

Here, too, Apple Pay's usefulness came from familiar consumer habits. By integrating into commonplace consumer technology that consumers were already using in their daily lives – such as on their iPhones and, later, on their Apple Watches – consumers could make purchases, dine out at restaurants, or take public transport without ever having to open their wallet or enter a PIN. With added security to the underlying payment process through biometric authentication – such as a fingerprint or facial recognition – users felt as though they could spend money safely in the future. By being deeply integrated with existing Apple technology, Apple Pay became integral to its ecosystem and sown the seeds for the large-scale adoption of contactless payment technology across industries.

PayPal and Apple Pay have shown and are still showing how digital payment is the way forward. It not only makes payments easier but also changes the very concept of trust and accessibility. They've both changed how we think about transactions, whether online or in the real world, and the possibilities for the future of digital finance.

2.2   The Growing Usage of Mobile Wallets

It's not just about credit cards and bank transfers anymore. With smartphones in hand, consumers now have another digital financial player: the mobile wallet. Ever slimmer than the original leather wallet that preceded it, this payment instrument stores information about a customer's accounts and allows the tap or scan of a phone or card reader to authorize a transaction. Mobile wallets are changing the way we handle money in ways that are so quiet they're easy to miss. Yet these 'digital wallet' apps are becoming essential tools for shopping, ordering a ride, joining a community loyalty program and much more.

2.2.1   Apple Pay, Samsung Pay, and Google Pay – The Main Players

Apple Pay, Samsung Pay and Google Pay are now at the forefront of the wider mobile wallet revolution. Despite the differences in each of these companies' digitization of physical commerce interactions, the common goal for Apple and the rest was to make financial interactions as secure, seamless and frictionless as possible. Apple Pay was the first of the companies to develop a physical-digital hybrid financial transaction stream that didn't require users to manually input account information or deal with a cashier. Apple's technology relies on Near Field Communication (NFC), which allows a consumer to tap their phone against an NFC-enabled card reader in a shop and complete a transaction. Launching in 2014, Apple Pay's tap interface represented the first major digital step toward making shopping an in-and-out experience. Samsung Pay launched less than a year later, and created a payment stream that could be used with a wider set of locations thanks to its support for both NFC and a technology called Magnetic Secure Transmission (MST), which simulates the swiping of a physical card. Finally, Google Pay's transaction streams allow a consumer to pay with a tap both in-store and online, as well as through in-app purchases.

The three brands are more or less the ecosystem of regulation and services that not only enable payment but also offer customer loyalty systems, rewards, or even transport services. They are moving the world away from plastic cards towards secure digital identities stored on mobile phones. The speed and ease spell the end of the wallet as we know it.

2.2.2 Mobile Wallets in Everyday Lives

Mobile wallets aren't just about paying for things; they're about creating a smoother customer experience. A single app can now store what your phone's wallet would have held: credit cards, loyalty cards, gift cards, coupons. No need to carry several pieces of plastic anymore – your loyalty program is an integral part of paying for something because mobile wallets integrate the process of payment and collecting loyalty points. For example, when you use Apple Pay or Google Pay at a coffee shop, you pay for your coffee and then automatically collect a stamp for your loyalty card.

Another force that has driven their success has been in-app payments. Whether you're paying for a subscription, buying virtual goods or ordering fast food, the payment process has been 'frictionless' enough that all you need to do is go to a screen and tap your fingerprint or stare into your phone's camera. The accumulation of these conveniences is making the mobile wallet seem like an everyday necessity – you don't need to think about it anymore than you do about tapping your debit card. It will just be there as part of your experience of interacting within the market as a consumer.

2.2.3 Geographical Trends - Dominance of Asian Countries in Mobile Wallet Initiatives

Although mobile wallets are taking off worldwide, Asia is leading the way and setting the pace in both adopting and developing these technologies. The payment ecosystems in countries across the region – in particular China, India, Thailand and others – have blossomed in the past few years to seize upon this trend. To illustrate the impact of mobile wallets, in China, approximately 82 percent of payments are made with a mobile phone; the Chinese mobile payment services Alipay and WeChat Pay are ubiquitous, and nearly every merchant – from street food vendors to high-end boutiques – accepts them.

India is another example, with cheap smartphones and explosions in the use of mobile wallet apps (such as Paytm and Google Pay) that offer hundreds of millions of Indians – and countless others around the world – a shifting menu of financial services, making transactions from retailing to health care, education to public transport available in countless rural locales where banks and ATMs. are few and far between. A smartphone becomes, in effect, a financial device.

This geographical leap – which reflects Asia's leadership in mobile wallet payments – isn't just telling us where consumer demand is keenest; it is also giving us a glimpse of our future way of paying for things, not just in Asia but elsewhere in the world. Once the technology matures and reaches scale, mobile wallets will just be there, as much a part of the payments world as cash has been in the past. And they will also be driving us, step by step, into the future of the cashless world.

2.3 Cryptocurrency and Payments

Cryptocurrencies, such as Bitcoin, have revolutionized the definitions of money and payments. There is no government that issues the money or authorizes its use – instead, digital money is issued by and managed with blockchain technology. Blockchain is a ledger that is spread out among all the participants in the network, meaning that everyone who participates in it 'knows' that the transaction is secure and clean. The notion of moving away from the type of currency we know – from the physical and centralized to the digital and decentralized payment tool – the idea of cryptocurrencies has created a variety of controversies as well as excitement. Payment in our everyday lives is a thriving industry in modern society, and, in many ways, it is a much better experience now than it was 20-30 years ago.

> ***Fun Fact:***
>
> *The first real-world transaction using cryptocurrency was for... pizza! On May 22, 2010, a programmer named Laszlo Hanyecz famously paid 10,000 Bitcoins for two pizzas. At the time, Bitcoin was practically worthless, but today, those 10,000 Bitcoins would be worth hundreds of millions of dollars! This day is now celebrated in the crypto community as "Bitcoin Pizza Day" – a reminder of how far cryptocurrencies have come in just over a decade.*

2.3.1 Impact of Bitcoin and Other Cryptocurrencies on Payment Methods

Cryptocurrencies first emerged with bitcoin, a niche form of digital currency that has been creeping into the mainstream. Bitcoin's decentralized nature offers people a means of exchange independent of banks and other financial middlemen – and, of course, an opportunity to trade with one another.

The most significant impact of Bitcoin and related cryptocurrencies, at least so far, is that they have provided users with a form of transaction that allows for fast, low-cost cross-border payments and has led businesses and individuals to use cryptocurrencies such as Bitcoin in ways and at volumes that could not have been achieved using traditional fiat currencies and associated payment mechanisms. More specifically, Bitcoin and other cryptocurrencies could potentially be used to address the problems of both currency volatility and weak banking access that are often associated with weak fiat currencies in developing countries. While there are many advantages of cryptocurrencies over fiat currencies, in practice, volatility has dampened the use of crypto for payments, along with associated regulatory uncertainty. Only a tiny fraction of payments have been made using crypto.

2.3.2 Businesses That Accept Bitcoin as Payment

Taking a cue from this popularity, a fair few companies now take Bitcoin too: Tesla is among the biggest names in this category after they began accepting it in exchange for vehicles a couple of years ago, a clear sign of how big corporations are starting to play with digital money. They stopped this after an outcry over its environmental effects, but it was still a signal that the currency could one day take its place in the modern consumer landscape.

Overstock.com, the online retailer, has also given customers the option of paying in Bitcoin. Although it is a small firm by Internet retailer standards, Overstock was one of the first major retailers to accept Bitcoin. It might be a sign that cryptocurrencies will disrupt the world of payments soon. Slowly but steadily, others, from small shops to service providers, are beginning to follow Overstock's example.

2.3.3 Challenges in The Crypto Space – Volatility, Regulations, and Security Concerns

Despite the multiple types of cryptocurrencies in the market today, there are still many barriers to overcome. The biggest problem is volatility. A currency like Bitcoin – and most other cryptocurrencies – can swing up and down wildly. It's close to useless as a currency when the price can go from, say, $2,000 to $4,000 to $11,000 in a week or lose much of its value in a day. A product that costs 1 Bitcoin today could cost much more or much less in a day and a half. No one can plan such a transaction or price such a product. Another problem is regulation. The rules vary from jurisdiction to jurisdiction, and a number of countries have yet to decide what kind of regulation they even want to level at this new kind of money. The risk of violating legal or regulatory mandates might be too great for companies to bear. Taxes might not have been configured correctly.

Thirdly, there is the issue of security. While blockchain technology is secure, exchanges and wallets, in which digital currencies are held, are not. There are many infamous incidences involving cryptocurrencies stolen; over the past few years, more than $74 million of digital currency has been lost via exchanges. Crypto theft will also affect confidence in crypto use payments. Businesses and consumers will need to take steps to feel confident about their transactions being safe and about their holdings not being hacked.

2.4　P2P Payments (Peer-to-Peer)

Today, we have widespread acceptance of peer-to-peer (P2P) payments. It lets us send money into an account without being tied to a traditional bank. It is due to the fact that the money is being paid directly and not via the banks that serve as middlemen in regular transactions. P2P payments are growing rapidly because they are easy to perform, with some of the most common uses being splitting meal bills with a group of friends or sending money to a friend in another city.

2.4.1　Venmo, Cash App, Zelle – Popular Platforms

Do you use Venmo, Cash App or Zelle? All of these are peer-to-peer payment systems that let you send money securely to another party without the involvement of a third party or bank – typically at zero cost to you. Venmo is the most popular of the group. In addition to basic payment transfers, it offers an array of social features that let you see what your friends are doing with their accounts. Venmo has turned payment into social, which is as much about connection as it is about transaction.

People are also signing up for Cash App because of its simplicity. You can invest in stocks or buy and sell Bitcoin within the app. Cash App is simpler than Venmo to use because it combines payments and investment-related expenditures into one system. This means you don't have to go back and forth between different apps.

Zelle operates like an app-to-app banking platform in a fairly seamless method since you don't need an additional app. You can send money from your bank account without having to use beyond your own banking interface. It is relatively fast, too. The average Zelle transfer takes about five minutes, making splitting a bill as quick and easy as it can be.

2.4.2   Instant Transfers and Bill Splitting – A Sociocultural Shift

One of the reasons P2P payment platforms have come to dominate modern banking is the fact that money moves between accounts nearly instantly. It used to be that sending money required a day or two for a cheque to clear or a special trip to the bank; now, all it takes are just a few taps on the phone to transfer cash. The fact that P2P payments are so quick means that day-to-day finance, especially those routine costs that need to be split, far more closely resemble pay-as-you-go. Bill-splitting, an awkward ritual at the conclusion of a meal, is now as easy as whipping out your smartphone and opening the Venmo or Cash App. No longer do pals need to scrape for spare change or decide whether someone can handle the bill on a credit card; the total can be split every which way, and payments can be made instantaneously to a digital wallet.

This change in how we manage money has larger social implications. The ease with which one can instantly settle a debt has smoothed the way for more activities in groups, shared expenses, and even lending money to friends without any shame. It is a reflection of a broader shift in how we think about money – away from cash and towards the act of instant transfer that makes everyday financial interactions effortless.

2.5   RTP – Real-Time Payments

Real-Time Payments (RTP) have the power to move money between consumers, businesses and financial institutions – and to move it faster than ever before. Transactions done by traditional fund transfers can take two to three days if not weeks. Using instant payments allows checks to clear within seconds. The benefits of speed are fairly obvious: it accelerates payments and increases efficiency.

2.5.1 RTP's Effects on Consumers and Businesses

RTP systems bring convenience for consumers making payments: whether you are buying a cup of coffee, paying a bill, sending money to a friend or colleague, or making a larger purchase, funds are debited from your account and credited to the payee's account instantly, enabling better cash-flow management. If you have the funds available, you can make payments when you need to, without waiting days for cheques or electronic payments to clear and then worrying about overdraft charges or other potential fees or having to wait until you get paid to transfer money into accounts used for paying bills.

Businesses benefit, too. Faster payment for merchants and service providers can mean better access to working capital, which can lead to better cash flow and improved efficiencies. For those companies that rely on near-instant payments, whether through a razor-thin margin or a high volume of daily transactions, better access to funds means a boon to the business model. For example, accepting payment by real-time transfer of funds instead of waiting for a paper cheque to clear stands to make a real difference. Owing to the decrease in operational activity, merchants can reduce overheads and focus on growing their business. Administrative tasks and fees related to the processing of payments that are currently tied up would also decrease.

2.5.2 RTP in the US vs. UPI in India – A Comparison

The United States and India have also stepped into this arena. The US RTP network, established by The Clearing House in 2017, allows any US bank to make instant payments between them and offers US consumers and companies a safe, low-cost and secure way to make payments between them. Its aim has been less to revolutionize the payment systems and more to account for the massive number of B2B and B2C payments that need to flow on a daily basis. The system has been slow to gain momentum as more banks and financial institutions adopt it despite the advantages of such a system. It has not yet achieved what we have witnessed in other countries.

India has failed to build on this success, but its own native digital payments system – via the Unified Payments Interface (UPI) – has exploded on the scene over the past few years to dominate domestic payments. UPI, introduced in 2016, enables any two bank accounts to transfer money in real-time – using mobile phones, without an associated banking app and without the need to download any other apps. Unlike other real-time payment systems, UPI is widely available and usable through multiple mobile apps to reach millions of users, including those in rural areas. It is arguably one of the biggest success stories of a real-time payment system in the world, thanks to government-led initiatives and the liberalization of rules to promote cashless payment.

Meanwhile, though the US RTP system is mighty, its adoption has been much slower due to the fragmented nature of the financial system and regulatory changes that financial institutions have been slow to implement. India's quick adoption of UPI shows how real-time payments can transform an economy and businesses alike.

2.6 Security and Regulations in Digital Payments

As more market transactions are conducted digitally, the question of trust in the reliability of this system – maintaining security and regulation of payments – is a pressing matter. The speed and ease of paying for goods online or via mobile devices are often highlighted as an advantage of digital payments, but there are also many associated risks, such as fraud or the misuse of private information. Some administrators and financial technology (FinTech) companies report that, in recent years, regulators have put a greater emphasis on working together toward the development of stronger regulatory protocols and enhanced encryption techniques in order to provide better protection for users' data and prevent fraud.

2.6.1 Regulatory Landscape Explained – AML, KYC

To ensure the security of digital payments, governments and financial institutions impose regulations on activities that can often be used for illicit purposes. The two primary regulatory schemes that govern this space are the Anti-Money Laundering (AML) and Know Your Customer (KYC) system.

AML rules are meant to hinder money laundering by spotting behavior that indicates shady financial activity and preventing illegally obtained funds from entering the banking system. Payment firms are required to report suspicious transactions and flag certain transaction patterns to ensure that they are not enabling criminal activity.

Meanwhile, customer due diligence (CDD), also called 'know your customers' (KYC), mandates that financial institutions and payment providers must know who's using their systems before transferring payments to them. If they want to know who their customers are, they will likely ask for identification, either a picture ID (typically) or proof of address documents (also typical), to understand who a user is. The KYC mechanism is in place to stop the system from being used anonymously by criminals and to prevent them from using the payment system as a vehicle for crime. AML and KYC are the two main pillars of regulatory compliance that prevent the payment system from being used illegally.

2.6.2 How Is Fintech Preventing Fraud and Securing Digital Payments

FinTech companies also often use cutting-edge technology in combination with user-friendly security measures, such as encryption, to stop payment fraud. This means that data such as credit card numbers and passwords are changed into a code that is inaccessible to other people.

Another major tactic is the use of multi-factor authentication (MFA). In this system, a user may have to enter two or more types of authentications before the system will allow access to an account or let a transaction through. An example might be a password paired with a one-time passcode sent to a user's phone. It's one more thing an intruder would have to infiltrate – in this case, the password plus the security on the user's phone – in order to make a fraudulent transaction.

Machine learning and artificial intelligence (AI) is also helpful to detect fraud by probing through vast stores of transaction data to look for anomalies – noteworthy patterns in real-time data flagging an individual as being far out of the normal behaviour range for that day and time and device and location. A payment initiated from an unfamiliar device or location could be flagged and stopped, for instance, or even queried back to the user for confirmation before being shut down.

Meanwhile, tokenisation can be used to improve the security of paying itself: instead of sending your card number to a merchant, for instance, tokenisation replaces that number with a unique identifier (the token) that can't be traced back to the card if it's intercepted.

Despite the prevailing criticisms – that FinTech payments are insecure, unregulated and vulnerable to criminal exploitation – security is front and center for all the new platforms and much of the new technology. For example, anti-money laundering (AML) and know your client's (KYC) rules are there to make systems safer for merchants and consumers. Digital payments might be coming of age, but the technology underpinning them will be developed continuously.

Adding 3D Secure Mechanisms

FinTech companies and payment platforms also rely on 3D Secure (3DS) to tighten the payment security even further. Founded by Visa and then adopted by Mastercard and other credit card companies, 3DS makes sure that the transactions are verified and approved by the cardholder. This helps in reducing fraudulent and unapproved transactions.

What Is 3D Secure (3DS)?

3D Secure was created specifically to secure online card transactions. It stands for 'Three-Domain Secure', denoting the three parties participating in its functionality:

1. Issuer Domain: The entity that issued the card, typically a bank or financial institution.

2. Acquirer Domain: The merchant's bank.

3. Interoperability Domain: The network managed by payment networks like Visa or Mastercard that facilitates communication between the payer and payee.

While conducting an online payment or transaction, 3DS requires the customer to confirm his/her/their identity before completing the payment.

This adds another strong layer of protection that helps identify the cardholder's true identity.

2.7   Future Possibilities in Digital Payments

The changes we'll see with future digital payments are likely to be even more disruptive than those of the past or present – although, judging by the current market, that means we're in for more volatility and new tech to upset the apple cart. Devices and financial technology are evolving very quickly, meaning that the way we pay will continue to change. Look at the potential of IoT devices or developments for cryptocurrencies – both of which could lead to another round of huge changes to payments.

2.7.1   Smartphones, Wearables – The Role of IoT in Payments

Digital payments already sit at the heart of the smartphone world, so we can safely assume that the next big innovation step will be in IoT. This might include smart watches, fitness trackers, smart glasses, and more as they become more actively involved in payments as part of our daily lives. More devices mean more payments will happen in the background as we go about our days.

Smartwatches such as the Apple Watch and Samsung Galaxy Watch already permit consumers to use the Apple Pay and Samsung Pay services to process payments at the point of purchase through a simple tap, making it far more convenient to pay without having to reach into a wallet or, indeed, without needing to have a phone at all. As IoT continues to grow, it is also easy to imagine other devices – including smart home assistants and even cars – becoming transaction-enabling platforms as well. Paying for petrol or groceries using voice commands or through touch in one's connected car might emerge as a widespread payment method in the future.

This IoT integration into payments will likely make it easier not only for consumers to buy but also for businesses of all sizes to transact with each other, making the entire financial output of the economy more automated and connected.

2.7.2 A Cashless Society and The Role of Cryptocurrencies in It – A Look into the Future

As digital payments grow in prominence, many experts predict that we will move towards a cashless society. In such a society, physical cash may no longer play a major role, with digital transactions becoming the norm for most types of purchases. The rise of cryptocurrencies is playing a major part in shaping this vision of the future.

Cryptocurrencies such as Bitcoin, Ethereum, Litecoin, XRP, Monero and others are already being used as a means of payment. They are not being widely used for day-to-day payments – mainly because of price volatility, regulation and security – but they will be adopted in time to replace physical currency as we know it today. This will make it even more likely that the long-discussed future of a cashless society will finally become a reality. Cryptocurrencies are an entirely digital form of money that is traded over the internet between transacting participants without the need for banks and other third parties. As cryptocurrencies become more stable and integrated into the global financial system, they offer a possible alternative to fiat currencies in an ever-more online world, a future that will become more online, even more so with the digitalization of payments.

Some have even started issuing their own central bank digital currencies (CBDCs), harnessing the efficiency of cryptocurrencies (speed, transparency etc) while retaining regulatory oversight and stability. Government-issued digital money offers a safer and more predictable alternative to decentralized cryptocurrencies and might hasten a cashless society. The world could be on the cusp of a future where physical cash plays a negligible, if not totally irrelevant, part – as some are predicting for Sweden – and where cryptocurrencies and other digital forms of payment dominate the global economy. Reducing the time, cost and complexity of conducting transactions will create new opportunities for populations that would otherwise have remained financially and digitally ostracised.

Final Thoughts

By the end of our digital payments and wallet journey, we can all agree that it is just about convenience and security and that technology is forging the future. From cashless payments to mobile wallets and cryptocurrencies,

Chapter 2 showed how the payments ecosystem is changing into digital and instant modes of transactions, allowing everyone to have the flexibility and control they need.

In the next chapter, however, we will delve into the next leg of FinTech – Open Banking – and discover how the latest developments in API-driven banking platforms allow financial institutions to open up their data to third-party developers and create more finely tailored, innovative and personalized financial services. Open Banking is about much more than the technology itself: it is destabilizing the relationship between customers and traditional banks altogether by carving out more power for the consumer and letting them take charge of their own finances. The third chapter will offer an in-depth overview of the advantages, challenges and potential of Open Banking as we continue to examine how financial innovations are shifting our relationship with money and further blurring the boundaries between banks and fintech companies.

Chapter 3

OPEN BANKING

Open Banking has completely redefined financial services. With Open Banking, you can allow third-party financial services and apps to communicate directly with your bank. It puts greater control of your financial life at your fingertips and a shift in power away from traditional financial services providers. It could enable you to easily access smarter budgeting tools, bring greater simplicity and choice in borrowing or investing, or make payments easier. By securely sharing financial data, open banking provides consumers and businesses with greater choice.

> **Fun Fact:**
>
> *Open Banking started as a regulation but turned into a global financial revolution! It was first introduced in the UK through the Revised Payment Services Directive (PSD2) in 2018 to increase competition and give consumers more control over their financial data. Now, thanks to Open Banking, you can manage multiple bank accounts from different banks in one app, access tailored financial products, and get personalized financial insights – all securely! Today, Open Banking is transforming how people interact with financial services across the globe, making banking more connected, flexible, and user-friendly.*

3.1   API-Driven Banking Explained

At the heart of open banking is the use of APIs: Application Programming Interfaces, or in other words software systems that enable different systems to communicate and work together. It's these APIs that allow any new service to get access to part of your financial data – with your consent – from, say, your bank.

An API is a bit like a drawbridge on the internet. Without an API, your bank's data is locked inside a faraway dungeon that you can enter only from the inside, either by going there yourself or having someone at your bank be nice enough to go there for you. If your bank offers an API, other applications can link to your account, and you may have the opportunity to enhance your financial activities. For instance, suppose you have installed a budgeting application that is capable of retrieving your transaction history in order to assist you in understanding where your money is being spent. For example, if you've downloaded a budgeting app, it can fetch your transaction history to help you see where your money goes.

This model represents a stark difference from the old world, in which banking systems were proprietary: you went to your bank to get a given service, and that was it. In the API-driven world of banking, rather than being held hostage to a singular proposition, you can choose from a selection of apps and services. You can have an app that helps you save money more efficiently or a tool that adds context and helps you find the right loan for you. It doesn't matter: APIs enable that information exchange and make it secure.

The biggest benefit of API-driven banking is choice. You get to choose which services are allowed to connect to your banking data – and, in return, those services get to offer you better tools to manage your money.

3.2   Successful Open Banking Platforms - Examples

Open Banking has been implemented across multiple places with great success. Examples include the platform Plaid that connects apps with users' bank accounts, such as the money-transferring service Venmo, the investment app Robinhood or the 'round-up' app Acorns. Through Plaid, a user can connect their bank account to an app, which allows them to move money, invest or save, all in one place.

Yolt, another player in the field, is a personal finance management app that helps you track your spending, set budgets and find better deals on utility or insurance by drawing on open banking data from multiple savings and transaction accounts and presenting this in a simple dashboard view, allowing users to manage their money without having to log on multiple times to different banks.

Monzo, an Open-Banking-built digital bank in the UK, offers a range of tools to help users track where their money is going. Customers can see their balances and live transactions, as well as use more sophisticated tools, such as saving pots and budgeting features. Monzo's Open Banking-based approach goes much further than what a traditional 'high street' bank would provide, as Monzo can integrate with other financial apps to offer better, tailored financial-planning solutions on its platform.

These applications are just a few examples of how open banking is being used to give people more choices, greater convenience, and more power over their finances.

3.3   Influence of Open Banking on Customers

What open banking ultimately enables is a new way for customers to manage their money. Through secure channels that pass data to and from different places, the idea is that you no longer have to have everything you need from your financial life in one place (e.g., one bank) because you can use a combination of multiple third-party providers via a portal of apps and accounts to create a financial toolkit that's uniquely suited to you. The power and capability are with the customer, allowing them to choose the service they want to have rather than one simply being thrust upon them.

This is enabling people to have a better handle on how they manage their finances through budgeting, saving or investment. In summary, open banking is helping the customer by bringing services closer to the way people live their lives, and their aspirations.

3.3.1   Open Banking Advantage: Consumers Can Personalize Their Finances

With the arrival of open banking, managing money is more of a question of 'what' rather than 'who.' Before open banking, most of what you could do with your money beyond what your bank offered you had to do with expert help – or in unsatisfying, semi-manual ways. Now, consumer-facing open banking apps make it easy to combine various current accounts with specialist data-crunching tools that help us to see and use our financial data on a real-time basis and can help shift behavior in ways that promise to save us money.

For instance, someone who is bad at saving gets an app that analyses their spending patterns and gives them specific suggestions on how to cut down on needless expenditures. Another person who is fixated on investment can use an app that tracks the market trends and also monitors their account balances to provide suggestions on when to invest. The end result is a more personalized approach that enables the consumer to make financial decisions on the basis of their current needs.

This ability to customize finance is a big change. It means that you can shape your financial future around your own habits, your income and your own goals, rather than in line with the needs of a bank that offers a one-size-fits-all service.

3.3.2 Apps That Use Banking Data for Budgeting and Finding Better Loan Offers

One of the biggest benefits of open banking has been the explosion of budgeting apps. Services such as Emma, You Need A Budget (YNAB), Mint and others use open banking data to explain your spending and income picture in real-time, not just tell you how much you've got in your account. They analyze your spending habits, categorize your expenses, and help develop a spending plan – providing advice in real time about how to best spend money according to your income while achieving your goals.

For example, by making it easy for users to attach their saving goals to categories such as rent, groceries, dining out, entertainment and so on, these spending trackers help them see more clearly where their income goes – and what they can do, for instance, about those unexpected recurring expenses that prioritize fashion over food. Some apps even let you link in multiple bank accounts, providing you with an instant snapshot of your financial health without having to run between different platforms. Many of these apps have features that will alert or otherwise prompt you when you're falling behind on any of your savings goals.

Open Banking has also made loan-hunting easier: sites such as Clearscore, Credit Karma and NerdWallet use banking data to offer customer-specific loan or credit card deals. You no longer need to spend hours researching lenders or Google, bookmark and enter your personal information on their websites – rather, your financial history is pulled from your bank (with your permission) and used by the platform to put your most promising offers at the top.

This is quicker, and also, due to the recommendations being based on your individual financial situation, likely to deliver you better loan conditions. Through this kind of service, consumers are able to compare offers one after another so that they don't have to guess whose offer sounds better, nor do they have to do all the legwork in order to find a loan.

Ultimately, open banking is putting financial management tools in the hands of consumers. People can use budgeting tips and deal-hunting for the best savings accounts or loans. The newfound access to this information should empower people to overcome financial hurdles, take back control of their financial future, and ensure that they can afford a happy and comfortable life.

3.4   Influence on Financial Institutions

While open banking brings a new world of opportunities for consumers, it also brings a whole raft of new challenges for financial institutions. When banks had full ownership over the data customers shared and the products and services they paid for, they controlled the landscape. However, with the advent of Open Banking, banks have seen their role profoundly interrupted. On the one hand, Open Banking's dynamic new environment has brought challenges; on the other, it has also brought opportunities to help banks recalibrate, innovate and find new ways to stay relevant in a fast-modernising new world of fintech and financial services.

3.4.1   Disrupting Traditional Banks

For many decades, traditional banks played a central role in the financial services industry: not only did they manage all customer flows and transactions, but they also were the only ones with access to customer data and that gave them the possibility to offer services ranging from loans to payments and financial advice based on such data. With Open Banking, this has completely changed: thanks to customer consent, third-party apps and platforms can have access to the same data and offer the same (or better) services.

The effects are unavoidable: if open banking allows a FinTech to offer a service that is quicker and more tailored than one provided by a bank, why should anyone bother visiting the bank in the first place? The answer is there really is no need to. The threat of a non-bank arriving to compete for banking services is enough to force an antiquated model that banks have had scot-free for a long time to innovate their services dramatically.

As technology companies start to offer financial services, banks are realising that they can no longer play the role of the 'middle man' as the primary 'pipes' to financial services, but must instead reframe everything they do with their clients – from sales to services – in an entirely new way.

3.4.2   An Opportunity for Banks to Renovate

Although the impact of open banking has altered the banking model and threatens to continually do so, the potential presents an opportunity for banks to modernize and make life easier for customers, a way to adapt rather than being fought by them. Some banks are going further than this, partnering with FinTechs or creating their own platforms.

Through Open Banking, traditional banks can offer improved, customized products. For example, some High Street banks are building their own apps that link to other financial platforms. In theory, this promises to make their customers' lives easier without them having to switch apps. Others use open banking data to create bespoke financial advice, loans, or budgeting tools specific to individual customers.

On the other hand, the models of open banking can help banks attract new customers – those who have previously been underserved. By partnering with FinTechs to offer various services, banks can extend their reach and appeal to a broader customer base, including those who prefer to use digital services rather than visit a branch. Whether it is keeping hold of existing customers or drawing in new ones, these changes bring benefits for banks.

In short, while open banking disrupts traditional banking, it also offers a way forward. Banks that are willing to adapt can find new ways to compete and thrive in this evolving financial landscape. The institutions that embrace innovation, improve their services, and collaborate with technology providers will likely be the ones that succeed in the long run.

3.5   Regulations and Compliance

Although open banking brings many advantages, it comes with the obligation to regulate how data is used in order to make it secure and private and to ensure equitable provision of services. Many jurisdictions have passed legislation and established standards governing how banks and third-party providers manage financial data, including provisions to enable data sharing in a safe and transparent manner and enable the consumer to control who can access their information.

3.5.1 PSD2 in Europe, Open Banking in the UK – Key Global Regulations

A cornerstone of open banking is the Revised Payment Services Directive (PSD2), enforced across the European Union, which mandates that banks open up access to third-party providers to the customer's financial data with the customer's approval. This means that third-party financial services can be used to innovate in a fashion that benefits the customer because the customer's data is the most important element and can be managed under the scope of assisting the customer. PSD2 also applies other rules in the movement of money to make sure that the money is getting there and is provided for so a customer isn't cheated or defrauded.

The same goal is served by the UK's open banking regulations. UK open banking enables a consumer to transfer a customer's bank account data to a regulated third party and then use it to access new financial services, such as a budgeting app on their phone or a personalized loan offer. This system – similar to PSD2 – is consumer-led, and the consumer decides which players can use their data.

These EU and UK regulations have since been adopted as the blueprints for open banking efforts around the world. Data security and informed consent, both assured by the enforceable requirements of these regulations, help make open banking safer, fairer, and more transparent for users standing to gain from it.

3.5.2 Data Security, Consumer Consent, Standards for Apps – Challenges Faced

Although there are quality regulations – such as PSD2 and the UK's open banking framework – there are still some great barriers to overcome. One is security. Financial data is highly sensitive, and a breach can have heavy implications for both the consumer and the institution. As a result, regulations require complex rules that must remain up-to-date with emerging technology – as they often do – to ensure the security of this data. However, hackers are also advanced, and so banks and regulators, as well as third-party providers, need to constantly keep an eye out to ensure the systems are up-to-date and secure.

A second key challenge is ensuring that consumer consent is clear and controlled. Open banking works through consumers giving permission for their data to be shared by their bank with other companies, but they have to give informed consent. In concrete terms, this means the customer must know what they are agreeing to and which services will use their data. The process can get tricky because this kind of data-sharing among apps is becoming more commonplace.

Lastly, there's also a need to ensure that apps adhering to open banking meet high standards of security and resilience. Regulators will need to challenge all third-party providers to ensure that they continue to keep their apps up to par, while protecting consumers against poorly designed apps or services that could mishandle the data entrusted to them. It's important that these standards aren't compromised by differences created by countries or entrenched platforms.

In the end, while open banking promises to provide great opportunities for both consumers and financial institutions, these challenges emphasise that security and trust are a prerequisite. The right equilibrium between innovation and regulation must be found, to allow consumers to be safe while enabling them to enjoy more tailored financial services.

3.6 Opportunities and Risks Go Hand in Hand – Security and Maintaining Consumer Trust

Open Banking offers enormous opportunities for consumers and financial institutions alike – but it also brings new risks, notably regarding data security and trust. The more access customers allow their financial information, the more responsibility falls on banks and third-party apps to secure that data. Trust between consumers and financial service providers is critical – if that trust is lost, the opportunities that open banking holds could be quickly overwhelmed by privacy and security issues.

On the plus side, open banking has driven the development of more tailored financial products, faster services, and better financial planning tools for consumers. People can manage money more easily, get tailored loan offers and use budgeting apps more effectively than ever before. And because so many more people have access to this level of financial data, financial institutions must demonstrate that they are capable of keeping that information safe. If they do not, then consumer trust could be fatally damaged, with the usage of open banking services being significantly downgraded.

One big hurdle is making sure that data is shared with consent and that all the parties involved treat it with respect. There are still plenty of people who aren't comfortable sharing their financial data and who would be alienated by misuse or any breach. Being able to get that balance right between the interests of users and those of the companies involved in open banking will be critical for everyone. The dangers could outweigh the benefits if it isn't.

3.6.1 The Potential for Traditional Banks and Start-ups

Open Banking offers significant opportunities for both traditional banks and FinTech start-ups, but they face different trade-offs as they attempt to enter this new market. For traditional banks, open banking is an opportunity to modernize and compete with more digital-first companies. Banks could invest in enhancing their online offering and partnering with FinTech start-ups in order to keep their existing customer base and reach new customers. They might develop new applications, such as more effective planning tools or faster and more transparent loan authorizations.

However, start-ups, without much in the way of legacy systems to maintain, can develop and market financial tools much more rapidly. They might choose to focus on even more narrow services, such as peer-to-peer lending or robo-adviser investment platforms, where they can offer a niche service, such as peer-to-peer loans or multi-asset funds that appeal to young, tech-savvy customers.

An open banking framework might enable start-ups to provide those services more efficiently, granting direct access to customers' accounts via real-time data and improving those services. However, both banks and start-ups will be forced to confront the same fundamental question: consumers must feel confident that their financial information will be secure. If people love a bank and its app, consumers will stick with it. But if they feel that their information is at risk, they will go somewhere else. In the case of existing banks, perhaps this means additional investment in digital security and making sure that your company's customer service is ready to respond to questions regarding data privacy. For start-ups, this means being able to show consumers that, despite its novelty, you are trustworthy and take consumer privacy and data protection seriously.

In short, both traditional banks and FinTech start-ups have a significant opportunity to grow by embracing Open Banking. Yet, they must focus on maintaining strong security measures and building trust with their customers. Success in this area will depend on how well they manage both the opportunities and risks that come with this new financial model.

3.7   The Future of Open Banking

The first change brought about by open banking is affecting how people engage with their money. There will be considerable changes over the next 10 years. More banks and FinTech companies building on open banking will further enhance their offerings, as will other parts of the financial services sector. The future of open banking should bring improved integration of financial services into the every day, more straightforward management of money, with more room for engagement for everyone involved.

In the years to come, technology will certainly transform our relationships with banks and with financial products further in that direction, towards services that are individualized, connected to real-time data, and virtually invisible, letting consumers make better financial decisions with less information.

3.7.1   The Impact of Open Banking on Financial Services in the Next 10 Years

Open Banking is likely to become standard in the next decade, as opposed to new or optional. It will be interesting to see how financial institutions refine their open banking offerings over time as they compete with each other. We might also see more collaboration between traditional banks and FinTech companies. Customers should expect more products, more personalized tools, and faster access to better services.

One obvious change would be the creation of integrated financial platforms – platforms that combine banking, investing, budgeting and lending into one simple consumer app. Whereas today, the average consumer uses multiple apps to access each of these financial services, a fully integrated financial app could allow users to view all of their accounts in one place, making it easier to track their spending, save money and plan for the future.

Artificial intelligence (AI) is likely to be a greater part of Open Banking's future, too. Increasingly, we will see AI-aided financial tools, providing consumers with better advice in real-time based on the data provided by their bank accounts. Such tools may help with everything from automated savings plans to real-time investment strategies. In the future, AI may be able to pre-empt financial needs, and advise you on products or services that could enhance your finances, based on how you spend and save.

On the client-side of things, open banking forces traditional banks to continue providing competitive digital services. If a bank is unable to keep up with the demand for fast and user-friendly tools, it could be left behind by more dynamic competitors. However, those willing to change and commit to new technologies might be able to create better services and stay in the game.

Consumers will face a similar security challenge as the volume of financial data between banks and third-party apps increases. Companies will have to continuously upgrade systems to safeguard customer data. This should encourage greater transparency and improve data-sharing standards – and trust between the consumer and provider. Open banking in the next decade will see more consolidation and much greater innovation as technology advances, along with how it enhances and becomes part of our daily lives, offering more innovative and tailored services. The winners in the space will be those who can balance innovation with security, offering every consumer the ultimate experience.

Final Thoughts

Open Banking is already transforming the dynamic between consumers and their banks, empowering wider access to finance, better consumer tools and better management of their financial data. It's setting the scene for a more agile, customer-centric and future-proofed form of banking. But that's just one aspect of finance's transformation. As open banking takes off, it'll start to interact with two other massive technological changes – both of which are set to bring more radical transformation to finance: blockchain and decentralized finance (DeFi). The next chapter will be about blockchain and how it is helping to map out a brave new world of decentralized finance and ways of managing and trading value. And how those forms of technology point the way for the future of financial services.

Chapter 4

BLOCKCHAIN AND DECENTRALIZED FINANCE (DEFI)

As we saw in the earlier chapter, Open Banking has revolutionized the relationship between individuals and companies with their financial data by giving control and mobility through secure data sharing. Yet, as we contemplate the future of financial services, another powerful trend is disrupting our approach to money, exchange and even finance itself: blockchain technology. Similar to how Open Banking allows consumers to engage in financial products in a bank setting, blockchain and DeFi will transform financial services by cutting out the middle man. With its decentralization of trust and peer-to-peer lending, blockchain is altering the financial landscape altogether. This chapter is about blockchain, how it operates outside crypto use cases, and how DeFi is breaking into financial services.

4.1   The Workings Of Blockchain

The term blockchain is already synonymous with digital transformation and there is good reason for that. Basically blockchain is an electronic ledger in which the transactions are held and stored on various computers. The thing about blockchain, though, is that it will not hand control over those transactions over to some central authority (a bank, say). Rather, it is decentralized, in which responsibility is evenly shared with everyone.

Each transaction on the blockchain is stored as a block, and once the block has been capped, it gets linked to the previous block – hence the name blockchain. This virtual chain is safer than an actual chain since it's impenetrable. Each new block is connected to the others by intricate cryptography, which means that information cannot be swapped or removed when it's inserted. Blockchain is so reliable because no one owns it, and tampering with it is nearly impossible.

> **Fun Fact:**
>
> *Did you know that the concept of blockchain was first proposed in a completely different field? The idea of a "chain of blocks" was actually introduced in 1991 by researchers Stuart Haber and W. Scott Stornetta to prevent tampering with document timestamps. It wasn't until 2008, with the release of Bitcoin's whitepaper by the mysterious Satoshi Nakamoto, that blockchain found its revolutionary use in digital currency. Today, blockchain technology is used not only in finance but also in fields like supply chain management, healthcare, and even voting systems!*

4.1.1   Distributed Ledgers And How Consensus Is Reached

A distributed ledger forms the foundation of blockchain technology. It is like a digital logbook that is not held in one place. Rather, replicas of this record exist in a huge collection of nodes or participants. Once a transaction occurs, it gets sent out to all the nodes in the network, and they refresh their own copies of the ledger. There's no central point for verifying the information with this decentralized system. The magic of blockchain lies in the consensus mechanism. So, in other words, how does one consensus determine what genuine transactions deserve to appear on the ledger? This is where the mechanism of consensus comes in.

Proof of Work (PoW), used by Bitcoin, is the most widely used consensus mechanism. In this model, the miners (participants) must solve a very tough math problem. The first person to guess the puzzle is granted permission to put the new block of transactions on the blockchain and gets paid accordingly. These puzzles require computationally high energy and computation, so they're secure because it would be incredibly expensive to attempt a cheat.

Proof of Stake (PoS) is another widely used model that requires little infrastructure. Rather than solving riddles, users in a Proof of Stake system are chosen to verify trades by how much crypto they own and are willing to 'stake' as collateral. The more you stake, the more likely you are to be included in the next block. This approach takes so much less energy yet also encourages validators to keep their heads above the water since if they undermine the system, they'll be out of a job.

Both mechanisms aim to make sure that all nodes in the network are on the same page regarding the ledger state. This common understanding enhances the system's security and reliability, enabling blockchain to function with no central office to monitor it all.

4.1.2   Supply Chain, Insurance, Healthcare – Real-World Applications Beyond Cryptocurrency

While blockchain was first built for the creation of cryptocurrencies like Bitcoin, its uses are not restricted to virtual money. Here are a few real-world use cases in which blockchain is already contributing. Transparency is key in the supply chain. Enterprises want to monitor items from source to end. Blockchain improves this process by making it more transparent, as each stage of the supply chain can be stored on a digital ledger accessible to everyone. Suppose you are buying coffee beans. You might be able to trace those beans through the production line, roasting and packaging steps, to the supermarket counter on the blockchain. Each transaction would be recorded on the blockchain so it could be trusted and used to fight fraudulent activity. That's trust — not only with the companies but with the consumers themselves, who require clarity of origin.

Insurance claims are notoriously slow and bureaucratic, taking countless pages of paperwork and rounds of verification. Blockchain can help make it easier by automating a lot of it. Suppose a smart contract (a computer program that executes on the blockchain) automates claims verification. Consider a policyholder's claim for an auto accident. The smart contract could verify that the claims process is complete (e.g., if the claimant has an active policy, if the accident was investigated by local authorities, and if the estimate of damage is correct). In case all goes well, the claim would be granted, and the money would be paid out by a machine without a human being having to act. This not only accelerates but also mitigates the possibility of scams.

Blockchain provides secure and efficient medical record management for healthcare organizations. Today, data on patients is not always coherent between different providers, and that leads to unreliable or deferred care. By blockchain, patient records are housed in one secure ledger and readily available to authorized parties. For instance, if a patient moves to a different city, their doctor might be able to see his full history on blockchain and administer proper treatment right away without waiting for paperwork to pass. Patients would also get to decide who has access to their information for more privacy and security.

These cases illustrate the fact that the scope of blockchain transcends cryptocurrency. It's a tech innovation that would alter the ways we exchange and validate data – securely, openly, and productively.

4.2   Cryptocurrencies Explained

We usually view Bitcoin and other digital assets as virtual currencies, but they are not exactly identical. Cryptocurrencies are digital tokens that utilize cryptography to authenticate transactions and oversee ownership. Cryptocurrencies function on decentralized networks, typically powered by blockchain technology, as opposed to traditional money controlled by governments and central banks.

This system offers a notable advantage: people are able to trade cryptocurrencies directly without depending on middlemen like banks, leading to faster and easier transactions.

Bitcoin, the leading and most well-known digital currency, established the foundation for this burgeoning online economy. Since it was created, many different cryptocurrencies have been launched, each having unique features and benefits. By grasping the concepts of key cryptocurrencies, we can delve into the workings of this advanced type of currency and understand its increasing appeal.

4.2.1   Bitcoin, Ethereum, And Other Alternative Cryptocurrencies

Bitcoin, created in 2009, is often referred to as 'digital gold'. It was designed as a peer-to-peer system for sending payments without relying on traditional banks or governments. What makes Bitcoin special is its limited supply: only 21 million Bitcoins will ever be mined. This scarcity, combined with growing interest, has driven its value up over time. People use Bitcoin for a variety of reasons, from speculative investment to transferring money across borders without high fees.

Then there's Ethereum, which is sometimes compared to Bitcoin but serves a different purpose. Ethereum is more than just a digital currency—it's a platform that allows developers to build decentralized applications (DApps). The Ethereum network is powered by its cryptocurrency, called Ether, which is used to pay for transactions and services on the platform. What really sets Ethereum apart is its support for smart contracts—self-executing contracts with terms that are directly written into lines of code. These smart contracts have opened up countless new possibilities, from decentralized finance (DeFi) applications to digital art marketplaces.

4.2.2   Adopting Cryptocurrency and Accepting Digital Currencies in the Banking Sector

Apart from Bitcoin and Ethereum, there are many other cryptocurrencies called altcoins. Some, like Litecoin and Bitcoin Cash, were faster or cheaper than Bitcoin. Others, like Cardano or Polkadot, try to go beyond blockchain and make it more scalable or interoperable. Each of these altcoins is different, but they have one thing in common: they provide an alternative to established economic models. Since cryptocurrencies have grown so popular, there are already a few banks and financial companies who are thinking about how to use them. The cynical reaction of big money towards Bitcoin was not the initial response, but with the development of crypto-currencies, it is. Now, more and more banks are experimenting with letting customers buy, sell, and own cryptocurrencies. In addition, some banks have already introduced custodial offerings that would store your crypto assets just like the old ones. It also proves that banks are starting to see crypto as an asset class that is actually legitimate and that they can provide it in addition to their other financial products.

Now, there is also growing interest in stablecoins, cryptos that are tied to an established currency, such as the US dollar. These coins deliver cryptocurrencies' features, such as low rates and fast transaction times, without the speculative volatility of coins such as Bitcoin. Others are even launching their own digital currencies, such as central bank digital currencies (CBDCs), which can facilitate faster and more efficient transactions under regulatory control. Adding crypto to banks is only a very early step, but things are moving. In the future, as the industry continues to develop, we will continue to see more banks providing crypto-based services to their customers and allowing them more control over their own asset management and development.

4.3   The Basics Of DeFi

DeFi, or Decentralized Finance, is the movement that wants to rebuild old-fashioned financial networks on blockchain technology without having centralized institutions such as banks or insurance firms. DeFi operates as an internal transaction between people, and all exchanges are under the control of smart contracts, self-executing contracts developed on blockchain.

> **Fun Fact:**
>
> *The value locked in Decentralized Finance (DeFi) was less than $1 billion at the start of 2020, but by the end of 2021, it skyrocketed to over $100 billion! DeFi platforms allow users to borrow, lend, trade, and earn interest on crypto assets without traditional banks or intermediaries. This explosive growth shows the massive interest in creating a financial ecosystem that is open, permissionless, and accessible to anyone with an internet connection – making DeFi one of the fastest-growing sectors in the crypto world!*

What makes DeFi exceptional is that it's also accessible. DeFi works for anyone with an internet connection; no gatekeepers are required. That offers opportunities for those left behind or excluded by conventional financial institutions. DeFi offers lending, borrowing, trading and insurance through decentralized networks.

4.3.1 Decentralized Lending, Exchanges (DEX), And Insurance

The key development in DeFi is decentralized lending. In conventional banking, banks issue loans. They hold your funds, check your credit, and determine if you qualify for a loan. DeFi, on the other hand, lets you lend or borrow from other members directly, all controlled by blockchain smart contracts. A bank does not need to lend the money — users can pledge the loan as collateral in the crypto currency, and the terms of the loan are pre-set by the contract.

The DeFi also has a crucial component of DEX or decentralized exchanges. In contrast to centralized exchanges (where the platform is run by a firm), DEXs permit participants to exchange cryptocurrencies directly. It processes the exchanges using smart contracts, so no middleman is required. This direct, peer-to-peer trading gives users more privacy and control. Likewise, DEXs are accessible 24/7, enabling anyone worldwide to get access anytime, anywhere, without having to create an account or share sensitive information.

DeFi insurance is not like that. Insurance is traditionally based on companies rating risk and making claims. In DeFi, it can be offered as insurance through decentralized networks that allow stakeholders to pool assets to protect against risks. They're smart contract-based, automating the claim so you get paid right away if the circumstances are met without an adjuster and with no lengthy papers.

4.3.2 DeFi Vs. Traditional Financial Systems

The key development in DeFi is decentralized lending. In conventional banking, banks issue loans. They hold your funds, check your credit, and determine if you qualify for a loan. DeFi, on the other hand, lets you lend or borrow from other members directly, all controlled by blockchain smart contracts. A bank does not need to lend the money — users can pledge the loan as collateral in the crypto currency, and the terms of the loan are pre-set by the contract.

The DeFi also has a crucial component of DEX or decentralized exchanges. In contrast to centralized exchanges (where the platform is run by a firm), DEXs permit participants to exchange cryptocurrencies directly. It processes the exchanges using smart contracts, so no middleman is required. This direct, peer-to-peer trading gives users more privacy and control. Likewise, DEXs are accessible 24/7, enabling anyone worldwide to get access anytime, anywhere, without having to create an account or share sensitive information.

DeFi insurance is not like that. Insurance is traditionally based on companies rating risk and making claims. In DeFi, it can be offered as insurance through decentralized networks that allow stakeholders to pool assets to protect against risks. They're smart contract-based, automating the claim so you get paid right away if the circumstances are met without an adjuster and with no lengthy papers.

4.4 Security, Regulations, And Challenges

For all the advantages of DeFi, there is a dark side to it. Security is never an option, since DeFi is based on blockchain and heavily uses smart contracts. Additionally, the regulatory framework for DeFi is still evolving, making things challenging for both users and regulators. This technology brings with it new possibilities, but it also brings new threats and unknowns.

4.4.1 Vulnerabilities In Smart Contracts And Hacking – The Risks In DeFi

DeFi's smart contracts are the heart of the operation. Such self-executing contracts are computer-programmed to perform transactions or enforce agreements without human intervention. However, smart contracts being coded are subject to bugs and vulnerabilities. If your smart contract is poorly drafted or doesn't account for certain circumstances, hackers can easily get at it.

The most popular is a 'code exploit', where a hacker finds a loophole or weakness in the contract code and takes advantage of it. There have been occasions when hackers have stolen funds from DeFi accounts due to such vulnerabilities. This is made even worse by the fact that DeFi is distributed and has no central management to come in and redo the transactions. And you can't get it back once the money is gone.

There are also the 'rug pulls' in which the developers build a DeFi project, coerce users to invest, and take off with the money. Since most DeFi projects are open source, customers cannot tell which sites are legit and which ones are scams. Despite these risks, there are ongoing efforts to improve the security of smart contracts. Audits by third-party firms, as well as tools that analyze contract code for vulnerabilities, are becoming more common. However, users still need to be careful and understand that DeFi is not without its risks.

4.4.2 Regulatory Hurdles And Government Responses To DeFi And Blockchain

DeFi's decentralized architecture presents an issue for regulators globally. Mainstream financial systems are governed by simple regulatory models that help to safeguard customers and maintain stability. DeFi, by contrast, has no central regulator, making the existing rules hard to enforce. Governments now need to figure out how to manage this new territory without inhibiting innovation.

What regulators most worry about is the treatment of fraud, money laundering and the misuse of funds within DeFi marketplaces. DeFi is anonymous, which makes criminal activity extremely hard to trace. Regulators are now starting to consider how to mandate AML and KYC on DeFi platforms, but mandating AML and KYC on a decentralized platform is not that simple.

Different countries have followed different paths. Others have taken up DeFi and blockchain, setting favorable rules to incentivize innovation. Other governments have been more sceptical, and have implemented stronger restrictions or completely bans on certain cryptocurrency-related practices. Because DeFi is global, regulations in one jurisdiction can influence the others.

4.5   Blockchain & DeFi In The Future

Blockchain & DeFi are relatively new, but are already generating waves in the financial industry. As such technologies develop, they will probably revolutionize how individuals spend money, transact money, and access financial services even more profoundly. The future is exciting as blockchain and DeFi can transform entire industries into an open, efficient, and transparent financial system.

4.5.1   Predictions For How Blockchain And DeFi Will Change Financial Services

Blockchain and DeFi will become a big part of our daily finance service over the next 10 years. Perhaps the earliest development we could see is a rise in blockchain-based financial products. DeFi could provide all the financial solutions without banks, from decentralized lending platforms to insurance and asset management.

The other prediction is that traditional banks will gradually adopt more blockchain-based services. Some banks have already started thinking of blockchain applications to enable cross-border payments and make it quicker to settle. The adoption can be reduced in cost, quicker transaction speed, and better financial settlement transparency.

On the user side, blockchain and DeFi can give people more control over their assets. Humans will be able to do these tasks without third parties who hold, move or invest money on their behalf. DeFi platforms will let users earn interest on their investments, transact assets, or even take out loans without going through a bank. The more user-friendly these services become, the more people will be able to sign up, and DeFi will become the default financial tool.

4.5.2   The Potential For Widespread Disruption

The explosion of blockchain and DeFi will cause a lot of unpredictability, particularly in the banking space. If DeFi platforms continue to gain momentum, banks could be more pushed around by users who move towards decentralized alternatives with better terms or convenience. Banks that don't move will lose their customers to these new, fluid platforms.

Insurance could be disrupted, too. These platforms become insurance distributed where users can collectively insure against a risk. This peer-to-peer model would compete with the big insurance companies, especially if it is cheaper or more effective.

Among them, perhaps the biggest disruption would arise in cross-border payments. Even now, overseas transfers via conventional channels are slow and expensive. Blockchain would make it simple so that payments will happen practically instantaneously with far lower fees. This would be great for anyone who needs to transfer money outside of the country as well as working with foreign customers or suppliers.

As blockchain and DeFi become mainstream, it isn't just in finance but everywhere else as well. We might even see decentralized infrastructure that handles everything from the supply chain to voting systems where we need trust and visibility. Because blockchain is distributed, it will be applicable to security and data integrity-intensive industries, so the usage is going to be far greater than what we're currently seeing.

Final Thoughts

As we have seen, blockchain and DeFi are already transforming finance, providing fresh opportunities to handle money, invest, and gain financial services. As they would lessen the need for institutions, save money, and make things more transparent, these technologies will bring even more transformation in the years to come. Yet the tale of finance innovation doesn't end there. Blockchain and DeFi are changing the landscape in one direction, but artificial intelligence (AI) is turning heads elsewhere, from fraud prevention to digitizing the banking system. In our next chapter, we'll look at the way that AI is becoming a driving force in fintech, transforming trading, improving customer experience, and posing new ethical concerns about finance's future.

ARTIFICIAL INTELLIGENCE IN FINTECH

As we transition from blockchain and decentralized finance to another influential power, Artificial Intelligence, technology is significantly changing the core of the financial world. While blockchain brought us secure, decentralized ledgers to potentially disrupt traditional finance systems, AI is enhancing this transformation with unexpected intelligence advancements.

While blockchain and DeFi introduced transparency and autonomy, AI focuses on efficiency, insight, and precision. Blockchain securely stores transactions while AI analyzes data to predict trends and risks and enhance customer experiences based on that information. United, these technologies are transforming the finance industry, yet they tackle it in varied ways: blockchain establishes a basis of confidence, while AI supplies the resources for more intelligent, quicker judgments.

In this section, we will explore the various ways AI is utilized in finance, such as streamlining tasks, improving the detection of fraudulent activities, revolutionizing customer service, and even impacting trading. Utilizing the advances enabled by blockchain, artificial intelligence is expanding beyond traditional limits to enhance finance, providing greater efficiency and personalized options for individuals.

5.1   AI in Finance Today

AI is now integrated into daily operations in the finance industry, silently enhancing various aspects such as customer service and risk management. Consider this—every time we access an application to verify a balance, settle a bill, or seek assistance from a virtual helper, AI is typically working behind the scenes, streamlining processes for all parties. This is not only about cutting down time for banks or financial institutions; it's about enhancing the overall ease and dependability of managing finances.

AI, or artificial intelligence, is a broad term. In the financial industry, machine learning technologies are used to examine past data, while natural language processing allows applications to understand and react to our questions. By utilizing these tools, banks and financial companies have been able to increase efficiency and enhance the precision and excellence of their services with fewer resources. For example, artificial intelligence has the ability to analyze large volumes of data to identify trends, anticipate dangers, and recommend customized financial solutions. These changes are not occurring in a distant future - they are happening now and influencing the functionality of finance in a practical manner.

Fun Fact:

Did you know that over 70% of financial firms use some form of artificial intelligence (AI) to improve their services? AI and Machine Learning (ML) have become game-changers in finance, helping banks and fintech companies detect fraud, personalize customer experiences, automate trading, and even predict market trends with impressive accuracy. Some high-frequency trading algorithms can make trades in milliseconds, far faster than any human could, by analyzing vast amounts of data in real-time!

A significant reason for the high importance of AI in finance is the substantial amount of data connected to it. Every payment, investment, or loan transaction generates data. AI intervenes in this situation, examining this information to understand it all, frequently in real-time. This indicates that banks and financial institutions are able to identify possible fraud, recognize patterns, and even stop problems before they escalate. AI-based systems could detect an irregular spending pattern and issue a warning regarding potential fraud before affecting a customer. This proactive approach has not only increased the efficiency of financial services but also enhanced their security.

AI also has an impact on customer service. Currently, an increasing number of individuals are utilizing digital channels to handle their financial matters, consequently anticipating timely, dependable assistance whenever required. AI-powered chatbots serve as an ideal illustration. These tools have the capability to respond to inquiries, offer recommendations, and assist customers in making financial choices, all without requiring human intervention. The constant availability makes it more convenient for individuals to receive necessary assistance promptly, bypassing typical wait times.

Providing a scale comparison, artificial intelligence has the potential to bring about substantial reductions in costs for the banking sector, with estimates indicating potential savings of up to $1 trillion by 2030. It is not only about reducing expenses; it also enables banks to concentrate on improving and developing services. By utilizing AI for repetitive, data-intensive tasks, financial institutions are able to focus on developing innovative ideas and improved solutions, ultimately providing customers with a more seamless and secure experience.

5.1.1 Is AI Taking Over Automating Processes, Detecting Fraud, and Improving Customer Service?

AI is entering various positions within the finance industry, revolutionizing day-to-day functions. AI is now automating processes, including routine tasks and essential security measures, that previously demanded significant manual effort and time. AI's capacity to handle routine tasks enables financial teams to dedicate more time to advanced tasks, enhancing overall efficiency.

AI is crucially impacting the automation of processes. In banks and financial institutions, numerous back-office duties, such as handling loan applications, organizing records, or synchronizing data, often take up a lot of time and are susceptible to mistakes made by humans. With the help of artificial intelligence, these tasks can be completed quickly and without errors. For instance, automation tools enabled with AI can quickly handle and validate transactions or documents, a job that could require a human worker for a significant amount of time. This sort of automation not only saves time but also boosts precision and dependability. Financial institutions gain advantages from efficient operations, while customers enjoy quicker, more seamless services.

Nevertheless, AI extends its reach beyond addressing tasks in the back office. Detecting fraudulent behavior is crucial in a society where online transactions are increasing. Detecting possible fraud in its early stages is crucial, and artificial intelligence is ideal for this job because it can rapidly examine vast quantities of data, efficiently pinpointing patterns and irregularities. For example, an AI system could examine a customer's purchase patterns and pinpoint any significant or unusual transactions that might suggest fraud. JPMorgan Chase uses AI-based security systems to safeguard customers and assets, offering fast reactions to possible dangers.

AI is altering the way individuals engage with financial institutions by enhancing customer service. Chatbots and virtual assistants, using artificial intelligence, can respond to questions, offer help, and support customers in making decisions. This is particularly useful when customers require prompt responses beyond normal business hours. Instead of waiting to talk to a customer service agent, people can get instant assistance from a chatbot designed to handle common queries and provide answers. These AI tools can offer tailored recommendations by examining account details, improving the personalized service provided, in addition to handling simple queries. Artificial intelligence is enhancing customer service by increasing speed, efficiency, and accessibility in multiple ways.

With these progressions, it is evident that AI is assuming essential positions in finance, not by completely replacing human employees but by improving their capabilities. AI enables financial professionals to concentrate on intricate strategic tasks, as it ensures operations run smoothly in the background. This type of equilibrium is enhancing the responsiveness and security of finance like never before.

5.1.2 Examples: Chatbots Powered by AI and Integration of AI in Personal Finance Apps like Cleo

AI-driven chatbots and personal finance applications are among the primary methods through which AI is transforming customer engagements within the finance industry. Let's examine in greater detail the functioning of these technologies and the reasons behind their significant impact.

For instance, chatbots have made significant progress. They are not restricted to basic Q&A conversations; they are advanced enough to grasp the context, identify particular user requirements, and provide appropriate responses.

> **Fun Fact:**
>
> *AI-powered chatbots are now handling up to 90% of customer inquiries for some banks, providing instant support and freeing up human agents to handle more complex cases. Thanks to AI, the finance sector is becoming more efficient, secure, and customer-friendly than ever before!*

In banking apps or on financial websites, these chatbots are available 24/7, assisting customers with tasks such as checking account balances and setting savings targets. They can even manage several conversations simultaneously, thus decreasing the wait times for customers who would otherwise have to wait in line or on hold. The consistency and reliability of chatbots are what makes them beautiful. AI-driven assistants are constantly accessible and offer a consistent level of service to all users, unlike human agents who may require breaks.

Now, think about Cleo, a personal finance application that utilizes artificial intelligence in a highly useful manner. Cleo not only serves as a budgeting tool but also functions as a financial advisor that can be easily carried around by users. Users are able to monitor their expenses, establish saving targets, and get advice on reducing costs in specific areas using Cleo. Cleo stands out by analyzing the financial behaviors of each user and offering personalized insights. Cleo can identify and suggest ways to better manage finances for users who tend to overspend on specific kinds of purchases. Providing individualized assistance like this would be challenging without AI since it necessitates the application to be able to comprehend and react to the distinct financial circumstances of every user.

In addition to budgeting, Cleo and other similar apps have begun incorporating AI tools that provide insights usually offered by financial advisors. Picture getting guidance on which expenses to focus on or even alerts before you surpass a budget cap. This is when AI proves to be extremely useful. AI-driven apps such as Cleo simplify the process of managing finances by using information on a person's spending habits to provide helpful advice.

These tools are making it easier to get financial services customized to individual needs. Chatbots and AI-powered applications enable individuals using smartphones to receive financial guidance, track expenses, and handle their finances without having to visit a bank or schedule a meeting with a financial consultant. These examples showcase how AI is affecting customers' finances by providing timely and relevant assistance.

5.2   AI in Trading

AI has completely transformed the way trading is conducted, particularly in major financial institutions and hedge funds where swiftness and accuracy are crucial. Considering it, trading has always involved gathering a large amount of information, analyzing it efficiently, and making decisions based on this analysis. However, with the increase in data and quicker market movements, traditional approaches struggle to keep pace. This is the point at which AI comes into play, equipping traders with the resources to make quick decisions using a vast amount of data.

Automated or algorithmic trading is a key manner in which AI is revolutionizing the trading industry. This involves more than just establishing certain limits and observing transactions take place. It involves developing systems that can quickly analyze and react to changes in the market, frequently making trades using numerous variables. For example, a trading algorithm using AI technology could analyze stock prices, interest rates, news articles, and social media trends. It takes into account all of these data points, analyzes them instantly, and then makes a decision to either purchase, sell, or hold—sometimes in a matter of milliseconds.

AI's impact in trading extends beyond simply being fast; it involves the process of acquiring knowledge and adjusting to new information. Using machine learning, these systems can improve their tactics as they adapt to shifts in the market landscape. Imagine a trading strategy that has been successful before suddenly becoming ineffective due to changing market conditions. An AI-powered system can identify this shift and adapt its strategy, a process that would require a human trader significantly more time to accomplish. AI's adaptive nature provides it with a unique edge in a rapidly changing financial market setting.

Predictive analytics in trading is further enhanced by AI's distinct layer of insight. Through the examination of past data and the recognition of recurring trends, artificial intelligence has the capability to predict future market shifts with a level of precision that was once unattainable. For instance, AI could recognize a trend where specific economic factors consistently impact stock prices in a particular manner. Equipped with this understanding, investors can predict these fluctuations and position themselves to profit, effectively staying ahead of the market. AI's ability to predict outcomes is why it has become a valuable tool in trading.

The outcome is a trading atmosphere in which decisions are not only quicker but also better informed. With AI, trading is based on data-driven insights and precision, not on guessing or gut feeling. Traders and financial companies have the ability to examine a greater number of factors, track real-time trends, and react immediately, providing them with a competitive advantage that was previously unattainable. Although human supervision remains crucial, the incorporation of AI in trading is resulting in a heightened level of efficiency and precision that is gradually transforming the financial industry trade by trade.

5.2.1 Hedge Funds Using Artificial Intelligence for Automating Trading and Market Analysis

Hedge funds have always looked for ways to act swiftly and gain an edge, and with the help of AI, they are successfully doing so. AI can be utilized by these funds to automatically execute trades and evaluate the market on a large level, managing data that would require human teams to handle much longer. This method is not only convenient but also changing how hedge funds function in the market. Let's analyze how it functions.

To begin with, AI enables hedge funds to engage in algorithmic or automated trading. This is where AI algorithms determine the optimal timing to purchase or sell depending on specific criteria. Picture a system that tracks price fluctuations, trade volumes, worldwide economic markers, and even the sentiment of news pieces to make instant decisions. If the information indicates a strong likelihood of making money, the AI will swiftly execute the transaction, typically in a matter of milliseconds. A human trader alone could not achieve this level of precision and speed. Once someone recognizes a potentially profitable trend and takes action, the AI will probably have executed the transaction.

AI involves more than just quickness. Hedge funds depend on the capacity of AI to learn and adjust. AI systems analyze every trade they make through machine learning in order to enhance their performance. Say an AI system from a hedge fund examines previous trades and discovers that specific market signals consistently result in successful trades. The AI consequently adjusts its standards, enhancing its ability to recognize those signs. With time, AI systems can improve their strategies, becoming more accurate and profitable. The benefit is that AI can adapt and improve with changing market conditions rather than being tied to one rigid method, resulting in increased effectiveness.

AI's ability to make predictions has proven to be highly beneficial for hedge funds as well. One example is when an AI system examines historical data and identifies a connection between a company's earnings report and its stock price fluctuation. This pattern is utilized to anticipate comparable movements in upcoming announcements, enabling the hedge fund to enter or exit positions at opportune moments. Aside from company profits, artificial intelligence could also take into account economic indicators, sector performance, and international happenings to forecast patterns, aiding hedge funds in forecasting future market directions.

Another advantage of AI in hedge funds is its capacity to consider the broader perspective while monitoring individual transactions. Unlike human traders, AI has the ability to monitor and analyze various markets and asset classes all at once without being limited to a specific set of assets or sectors. This comprehensive assessment allows hedge funds to vary their tactics, spreading out risks among different sectors and discovering new possibilities as they arise. AI enables hedge funds to be more adaptable and quicker in adjusting their portfolios, surpassing the capabilities of traditional methods.

This signifies that hedge funds utilizing AI are ready to react quicker, adjust more effectively, and make wiser choices. They can identify opportunities that others may overlook, providing them with a strong edge in a fiercely competitive industry.

5.2.2 Ethical Concerns Regarding AI-Driven Trading Decisions

The quick growth of AI in trading has raised various ethical concerns that surpass basic technical inquiries. These concerns center on equity, accountability, and financial stability, which are crucial elements impacting all participants in finance, including big corporations and individual investors. Let's delve deeper into these.

Fairness is a significant concern. Developing and maintaining AI-driven trading systems can be costly, limiting access to primarily large firms with ample financial resources. This provides these companies with a benefit as their artificial intelligence can conduct trades more quickly and respond to information that is challenging for smaller traders to obtain. For instance, an artificial intelligence algorithm could identify a pattern and execute a trade within a split second, ensuring a more favorable price. On the flip side, smaller companies and independent investors may overlook these chances due to lacking access to similar resources. This poses the question: is it just for only the richest players to profit from this technology while leaving others in the dust?

An additional significant concern is the possibility of disruptions in the market. AI systems engaging in rapid trading with large amounts of transactions can lead to abrupt changes in the stock market values. This might result in a 'flash crash', causing prices to drop briefly before stabilizing. These sudden drops can be alarming and result in actual financial setbacks for those affected. During a sudden market drop, a small investor could become fearful and quickly sell their stock at a reduced price, believing the market will decline, only to witness the price rise again shortly thereafter. These events demonstrate the potential market destabilization caused by AI high-frequency trading, even if temporary.

Transparency is also an important issue. AI-powered systems, in contrast to human traders, usually depend on complex algorithms that can be hard for even their designers to understand, making it difficult to justify their strategies. It is difficult to attribute fault or accountability in a situation with insufficient transparency. Who is responsible when an AI system causes an error or executes a trade that leads to substantial financial setbacks? Which company utilizes artificial intelligence? Who was responsible for its development? Is it the AI system itself? These questions are complex, and at the moment, there are no definite answers available. The absence of responsibility can result in scenarios where nobody assumes accountability, which is particularly worrying when significant amounts of money and financial security are involved.

Regulators are beginning to investigate the use of AI in trading, and some are suggesting regulations to promote fair usage in response to these challenges. This may involve making companies disclose more about how their AI systems function or placing restrictions on the speed and quantity of trades AI is capable of conducting. The objective is to stop AI from fostering an unjust market atmosphere or leading to unintended outcomes. Although these rules are still developing, they aim to achieve a balance between the advantages of AI in trading and the importance of fairness and market stability.

These ethical issues serve as a reminder that AI's role in increasing trading efficiency also entails certain responsibilities. As we increasingly depend on AI for financial choices, it is important to tackle these issues to guarantee that technology benefits everyone equitably and responsibly.

5.3   AI and Fraud

Identifying and stopping fraudulent activities is a major focus in the financial sector, and artificial intelligence plays a crucial role in tackling this problem. Every day, financial institutions handle high amounts of transactions, subjecting themselves to ongoing risks from fraudsters looking to exploit any weaknesses. Historically, fraud detection depended on human-created rules, such as identifying transactions exceeding a specific value. However, AI now allows banks and financial institutions to identify patterns and detect potentially fraudulent activities with greater precision and speed.

The strength of AI in detecting fraud lies in its capacity to analyze vast quantities of data instantly. AI differs from conventional approaches in that it examines not only individual transactions but also analyzes trends in a customer's complete purchase record and contrasts these trends with numerous others, looking for any anomalies. If someone typically makes small buys but then suddenly makes a big purchase in a different country, AI could see it as questionable. The reason for this is not one specific rule but rather AI's identification that this activity deviates from the customer's typical spending patterns.

AI not only identifies fraud but also anticipates potential threats in order to prevent it. By utilizing machine learning, artificial intelligence can analyze previous cases of fraud to recognize common patterns and behaviors associated with fraudulent actions. Teaching AI to distinguish fraudulent behavior is similar to training a dog to recognize specific odors; when AI identifies fraud, it can react appropriately. This proactive method enables financial institutions to anticipate and prevent suspicious transactions before they are completed.

5.3.1   Usage of AI in Detection and Prevention of Fraud

AI is crucial in identifying and stopping fraud. In a constantly evolving landscape of financial crime, banks gain a competitive advantage through AI's real-time data monitoring and analysis capabilities. Let's analyze the practical application of AI in combating fraud.

AI excels in examining behavior as a crucial area. Every individual has a distinct behavior when it comes to spending, withdrawing money, or moving funds. AI monitors these patterns, establishing a profile of the typical behavior of each individual. If something does not fit this profile, AI marks it for further examination. If a customer usually buys things within a specific amount and then suddenly splurges in another country, AI will notice this anomaly and inform the bank. It is challenging to attain such a high level of precision through human supervision, especially considering the quick response needed to thwart fraud in advance.

AI is also highly useful in analyzing trends among numerous accounts. Fraudsters typically target multiple accounts instead of focusing on just one in order to avoid detection. AI systems are able to identify these patterns through the analysis of data from various accounts. When AI detects the same unusual transactions occurring across several accounts, it can identify it as a possible fraud plan and notify security teams. This is particularly useful in stopping extensive fraudulent activities that could bypass conventional detection methods.

AI's effectiveness in fraud prevention is largely due to its ability to constantly learn and adapt. AI adjusts by examining fresh data from recent incidents as fraudulent tactics advance. This enables it to identify novel methods and tactics employed by criminals. Picture a scenario in which a team of hackers discovers a fresh method of pilfering data and leverages it to carry out fraudulent activities. AI can analyze, learn from, and adjust its detection methods based on these cases, making it harder for similar scams to succeed in the future.

5.3.2   Example: How Large Banks Like JPMorgan Use AI for This

Large financial organizations like JPMorgan Chase have invested heavily in artificial intelligence to improve their capabilities in spotting and stopping fraudulent activities. Having AI systems in place is almost essential due to the large volume of transactions they handle daily.

JPMorgan utilizes AI to observe transactions in real-time, identifying anything that seems questionable. If the system notices an abrupt increase in withdrawals from a customer's account or numerous transactions happening rapidly in various places, it will trigger a warning. This happens within seconds, enabling the bank to stop the transaction, contact the customer, and verify if the activity is genuine. This rapid reaction time is essential for stopping fraud before it impacts the customer's financial situation.

AI also contributes to enhancing customer trust and experience at JPMorgan. AI prevents fraudulent transactions to help customers avoid the hassle of disputing charges or managing a depleted bank account. The precision of the system results in a lower number of false positives, reducing the instances of legitimate transactions being incorrectly identified as suspicious, leading to a more streamlined overall experience. Customers can trust in the bank's security without experiencing frequent interruptions in their usual banking transactions.

JPMorgan utilizes AI to team up with different data sources and systems in order to stay ahead of upcoming threats. For instance, AI models have the ability to examine information from different banks and institutions, ensuring that JPMorgan stays informed about emerging fraud tactics in other places. This collective knowledge enables JPMorgan's AI to more effectively anticipate and thwart comparable fraud schemes, guaranteeing that they are not surprised by new strategies.

The continuous evolution of AI in the finance industry presents ethical concerns impacting different parties, such as individuals, financial institutions, and governments. The impressive benefits of AI, including quickness, effectiveness, and flexibility, pose obstacles that should not be ignored. These obstacles are especially crucial in the field of finance, as choices impact individuals' lives, their ability to obtain resources, and their overall financial health. It is crucial to evaluate AI not just for its capabilities but also for its responsible and fair use.

Three major concerns in AI currently include bias, transparency, and privacy. Every one of these domains poses inquiries regarding trust, accountability, and security, which are crucial for upholding faith in AI-driven financial services. Partiality, such as bias, could result in unequal treatment of specific groups, resulting in unjust results in loan approvals, credit scoring, or investment suggestions. Transparency, on the contrary, deals with how AI determines outcomes and if users are entitled to comprehend those procedures. Privacy issues are centered on the large quantity of personal data that AI systems analyze and how this data is safeguarded.

Ethical concerns are increasing as AI becomes increasingly prevalent in finance. Financial institutions and regulators understand that not addressing these problems could result in mistrust and harm, affecting both clients and the financial system as a whole. It is essential to tackle these challenges in order to maintain the positive impacts of AI while also upholding fairness, accountability, and privacy.

5.4.1   Addressing Issues Like Bias, Transparency, and Privacy

To begin with, let's talk about bias. AI systems gain understanding from data, and if the data contains biases, the AI could unknowingly propagate them. In the financial industry, this may lead to certain groups experiencing unfair disadvantages in loan approval or credit scores. If an AI system is trained with past data that indicates certain groups had lower loan approval rates, it could unknowingly continue this inequality. This raises a major moral quandary: how do we guarantee that AI treats every person fairly? Many financial institutions are currently working on eliminating this bias by testing and refining their algorithms, but it remains a field that needs ongoing oversight.

Transparency remains another important concern. AI models, especially those employing sophisticated machine learning techniques, often operate as an enigmatic entity that makes it difficult to understand the reasoning behind its decisions. In the finance sector, a lack of clarity can lead to issues with accountability. Customers may wish to understand the reasoning behind AI's choice to deny a loan or flag a transaction as questionable. However, explaining AI choices may prove to be difficult, even for the developers in charge of creating the model. Lack of transparency can lead to customers feeling unsure or unfairly handled, particularly when choices affect their financial well-being. Financial institutions are currently looking into methods to increase transparency in their AI systems by providing explanations for customers to comprehend the reasoning behind decisions.

Next comes the matter of privacy. Financial institutions are utilizing AI to analyze vast quantities of individual data to offer services and prevent fraud. However, as more data is gathered, more issues arise regarding who can access it and the manner in which it is utilized. Customers may have concerns about their financial behaviors being monitored too closely or their information being shared without permission. In order to address these issues, numerous banks and financial institutions are putting resources into more robust data security measures. This involves restricting data access to individuals who require it and guaranteeing secure storage of sensitive information. Privacy is not solely a technical concern; it revolves around the trust established between financial institutions and their clients.

5.4.2   The Efforts of Regulators to Address These Concerns

Regulatory bodies globally are closely monitoring these ethical concerns, recognizing the importance of overseeing AI's influence on finance to promote fair and accountable practices. Multiple nations have already started creating rules and regulations regarding artificial intelligence, particularly concerning fairness, transparency, and data privacy. For instance, certain governments are developing legislation that mandates financial institutions to clarify their AI-based decisions to customers, guaranteeing that individuals comprehend how their data is utilized and the reasoning behind particular decisions.

Furthermore, there is an increasing demand for 'AI audits' in which third-party entities evaluate the algorithms employed by financial institutions to examine potential problems such as bias and fairness. These assessments can pinpoint areas where AI systems may require modifications to prevent unintentional biases from being reinforced. Regulators aim to establish a system where AI promotes financial fairness instead of inadvertently compromising it by ensuring these checks.

On the privacy front, numerous regulators are advocating for more robust data protection laws that specifically target AI systems. These rules aim to ensure that customer data is managed in a responsible manner by restricting the amount of information gathered and guaranteeing secure storage of data. In the European Union, the GDPR already sets strict rules for data management, and other regions are also looking into implementing similar measures to protect customer data in AI-powered settings.

Final Thoughts

As observed, AI has significantly altered the finance sector; however, it carries responsibilities that are equally crucial to its advantages. Making sure AI systems are fair and transparent and protect privacy is crucial for earning the trust of the individuals these systems cater to, not just for regulators and financial institutions. When creating an advanced and fair financial system, it is crucial to carefully consider the advantages of AI in comparison to ethical concerns.

Considering this, our attention will shift to Central Bank Digital Currencies, commonly referred to as CBDCs. AI is changing how we engage with financial services, but CBDCs have the power to completely change the essence of money. When looking at CBDCs, we will analyze how central banks are adapting to the digital age, possibly creating novel forms of currency that can complement AI technology for innovative financial solutions.

Chapter 6

CENTRAL BANK DIGITAL CURRENCIES (CBDCs)

As we move forward from exploring the impact of AI in finance, it is clear that the realm of financial technology is growing in various ways. We have witnessed the way AI changes trading, fraud detection, and customer interactions, leading to opportunities and ethical debates. However, as AI continues to influence the operations of financial services, another idea is becoming more popular and changing our perspective on money: Central Bank Digital Currencies (CBDCs).

CBDCs, unlike traditional physical money or online transactions, are created to serve as a digital version of a country's money, controlled and distributed by the central bank. This is not only about enhancing transaction efficiency but also about reconfiguring the monetary system to match contemporary financial behaviors and the digital economy. The emergence of CBDCs presents a combination of possible advantages and fresh obstacles, impacting not only the public but also conventional banks and financial institutions. In order to grasp this new digital currency trend, it is crucial to differentiate CBDCs from cryptocurrencies, explore their current testing

> ***Key Facts and Predictions (2024-2030):***
>
> *By 2026, over 50 countries are expected to have fully operational CBDCs, with a focus on Africa, Asia, and Europe.*
>
> *The global market for CBDC-related infrastructure is forecasted to reach $200 billion by 2030, driven by investment in blockchain, cloud, and cybersecurity.*
>
> *Cross-Border Payments: The Bank for International Settlements predicts that CBDCs could reduce cross-border payment costs by up to 50% by eliminating intermediaries.*

in different regions, and consider their potential impact on banking and financial inclusivity.

6.1 Understanding Central Bank Digital Currencies (CBDCs)

CBDCs are digital currencies that are created and handled by a country's central bank. Central bank digital currencies, in contrast to cryptocurrencies, receive backing from the central bank and function in a centralized fashion. This is why they exhibit less volatility compared to traditional currencies. In place of physical currency, virtual alternatives bring advantages like better financial service availability, simple transactions, and increased protection from fraud.

Central bank digital currencies are issued in different ways, depending on which central bank issue it. Some digital currencies are open to the public (retail CBDCs), and others are only open for payment by banks (rich CBDCs). The privacy aspects of such systems can range from total transactional anonymity to the ability to trace each transaction. Every system attempts to maintain privacy without being controllable, as central banks prefer.

Fun Fact:

CBDCs are designed to be as secure and stable as cash, but unlike cash, they allow central banks to implement policies like interest-bearing digital money. This could mean that in the future, central banks could use CBDCs to implement new forms of monetary policy directly with citizens, such as stimulating spending by offering "expiring" digital currency!

In 2022, the Bank for International Settlements (BIS) reported that over 80% of central banks across the world were in the process of researching or creating CBDCs. The mass popularity of crypto indicates a shift in perception among nations, which is evident from the latest reports, which indicate that over 130 countries are actively developing CBDCs. CBDCs aim to offer consumers a secure digital alternative to paper money in the hope of superseding cash rather than upending it like cryptocurrencies. These benefits might range from increased financial services for non-bank customers, faster and cheaper payments, and enhanced protections against faking money.

6.1.1 The Distinction Between CBDCs and Cryptocurrencies

CBDCs and cryptocurrencies are digital currencies but have some differences. Both Bitcoin and Ethereum run on decentralized networks with no control from a central entity. This freedom can create differences in price and unpredictability. Central Bank Digital Currencies, however, are issued and controlled by a country's central bank, offering them the security associated with fiat money.

Central bank digital currencies provide a bridge between traditional paper money and electronic finance transactions. They strive to maintain trust and safety through their inclusion in the centralized monetary system, ensuring that they are as valuable as real currencies. In contrast, cryptos are typically considered to be speculative assets and, therefore, might not be purchased regularly.

6.1.2 Examples: China's Digital Yuan, The Bahamas' Sand Dollar, and The European Central Bank's Digital Euro

Many countries are exploring or utilizing CBDCs to different degrees and with different methodologies and maturity levels.

➤ **China's Digital Yuan (DCEP):** The People's Bank of China has made significant efforts to implement the DCEP in China. One of the first industrialized nations to test CBDC was China. In 2023, the DCEP pilot project generated more than 70 billion yuan (\$10.9 billion) in transaction volume from cities around the world. China's success in developing and testing CBDCs has encouraged other countries to emulate it.

- ➤ **The Bahamas' Sand Dollar**: It wasn't long before The Central Bank of The Bahamas digitalized the Bahamian Sand Dollar. In this move, The Bahamas became one of the first states to introduce a CBDC. The Sand Dollar was introduced to foster greater financial inclusion for those without access to banks in the countryside. Transactions and use of financial products are safe and efficient using this platform.

- ➤ **The European Central Bank's Digital Euro**: The ECB has been investigating the possibility of creating a digital euro. The ECB has organized public workshops and conducted scientific experiments in an attempt to uncover the advantages and disadvantages. The ongoing research and negotiations have led to the European commitment to digital solutions in the eurozone in 2023, despite the final outcome being a year away.

- ➤ **The Bank of England's Digital Pound**: The Bank of England has also done the same. The organization has released papers and engaged in discussions with the public on the feasibility and potential impact of implementing a digital pound. As of 2023, there is still no conclusive decision regarding the full integration of a CBDC.

These instances demonstrate the varying approaches central banks are taking towards developing CBDCs. While The Bahamas has already introduced its digital currency, others are still in the process of investigating the possible advantages and drawbacks. Countries like China are making advancements in large-scale trials, which indicates the increasing significance of CBDCs in modern financial systems. This new era of exploration and progress is changing the way individuals can engage with money in the upcoming years, combining the reliability of traditional banking with the ease of digital transactions.

6.2   Impact on Traditional Banking

Banks are now being urged to shift towards utilizing Central Bank Digital Currencies, known as CBDCs. The arrival of these newcomers will drastically alter the way commercial banks operate, their interactions with customers, and the central bank.

6.2.1 Possible Impact of CBDCs on Commercial Banks

CBDCs threaten the disintermediation of commercial banks. It is hoped that allowing individuals and firms to make deposits directly into the central bank will also drive them away from large deposits at commercial banks. This can be disruptive to the industry and affect banks' ability to repay loans and cash out assets. In a recent OMFIF survey, two-thirds of central banks believe they will be disintermediated if they implement CBDC.

The ability of CBDCs to transform current payment systems is found in their efficiency and security. The conventional banking system depends on multiple middlemen, leading to possible delays and costs. Central Bank Digital Currencies (CBDCs) make processes more efficient, leading to faster and more efficient transactions. Payment systems that are operational 24/7 will be increasingly accessible and aligned with customer needs.

Moreover, Central Bank Digital Currencies could create new opportunities for monetary policy. Central banks could choose to influence the economy by changing the interest rates on CBDCs through policies. For example, they could impose or offer interest on digital assets to regulate economic transactions. This could provide central banks with an additional instrument in their policy arsenal, enabling more precise economic interventions.

6.2.2 Advantages of Financial Inclusion and Improving Transaction Efficiency

One important advantage of CBDCs is their ability to improve financial inclusion. In numerous areas, individuals lack the means to access traditional banking services. A CBDC issued by and backed by the central bank could provide a secure and simple way for individuals without bank accounts or with restricted banking services to access the digital economy. This may decrease the number of people left out of financial services and create chances for a more encompassing economic expansion.

CBDCs could also improve effectiveness in transactions. Reducing the number of intermediaries needed for payments could lead to faster and more economical transactions. This advantage also benefits businesses by enhancing cash flow and enabling more streamlined operations through decreased transaction fees and faster processing times. The increased effectiveness would help create a financial system that is more adaptable to the pace and requirements of contemporary business.

Nevertheless, there are challenges involved in the implementation of CBDCs. Properly addressing technical challenges, cyber threats, and privacy issues is crucial to ensure the safety and efficiency of these digital currencies. Cyber threats are highly risky as they can impact both individuals and entire financial systems. Central banks will face a significant challenge in balancing transparency and privacy when implementing these digital solutions.

Certain suggested CBDCs, such as the digital euro, are investigating a 'tiered remuneration' system. This system enables digital assets below a specific threshold to generate interest, while amounts exceeding this threshold may not earn interest or could even incur negative rates. This would allow central banks to more effectively control the circulation of money and deter the practice of hoarding. Central Bank Digital Currencies offer advantages and drawbacks for the traditional banking industry. Careful planning and secure implementation will be crucial in ensuring the success of these new tools for monetary policy, promoting financial inclusion, and enhancing transaction efficiency.

6.3   Challenges to CBDC Adoption

The idea of CBDCs has significant promise, but there are various challenges in their implementation that require close consideration. The obstacles consist of technical problems, privacy issues, security threats, and finding the right mix of government control and decentralization.

6.3.1   Technical, Privacy, and Security Challenges

Creating a technical system that can support the widespread use of CBDCs on a national or global level is a significant challenge. Guaranteeing the efficient operation of digital currencies requires reliable, strong systems able to quickly and securely handle high transaction volumes. To keep the system operating smoothly, a substantial investment in technology and continuous updates is necessary. For example, China's Digital Yuan has set a benchmark by developing a solid infrastructure that can handle up to 300,000 transactions per second.

Concerns about security risks are significant as well. Just like all digital systems, CBDCs might be at risk of cyberattacks. An IMF report from 2023 stated that cyberattacks targeting CBDCs had gone up by 25%. A breach may result in significant repercussions, ranging from theft to disturbances in the financial system. Defending against such dangers requires robust cybersecurity protocols and ongoing attention to adjust to changing cyber threats.

Privacy is yet another intricate matter. Surveys show that a massive 72% of Europeans are concerned about a lack of privacy when it comes to CBDC transactions. Although CBDCs have the potential to enhance transparency in financial transactions, they may also lead to increased government monitoring of people's spending behaviors. This brings up concerns regarding the level of privacy individuals would have in their financial transactions. The delicate task that central banks must handle is finding a balance between financial privacy and transparency. Certain suggestions propose the inclusion of choices that enable different levels of transaction traceability to tackle these privacy issues.

6.3.2   Government Control vs. Decentralization

Central Bank Digital Currencies are closely monitored by the government, in contrast to the decentralized structure of cryptocurrencies. This sparks discussions on the consequences of authority, management, and personal liberty within financial systems. Supporters claim that a centralized body overseeing CBDCs can guarantee stability and decrease financial offenses such as money laundering. Nevertheless, critics are concerned that digital currencies issued by central banks may lead to heightened surveillance and diminished financial independence for individuals.

To tackle these issues, certain nations that are creating CBDCs, like the digital euro, are examining concepts such as 'tiered remuneration.' In this setup, only a specific quantity of CBDC holdings would earn interest, which would discourage excessive transfers from commercial banks to central bank accounts. Actions such as these seek to find an equilibrium between fostering innovation and upholding a steady financial environment.

The emergence of CBDCs creates potential advantages as well as obstacles. While they pledge to enhance transaction efficiency, provide new monetary instruments, and promote financial inclusion, they also present technical, privacy, and security challenges that need to be resolved. Achieving the right equilibrium between government regulation and individual freedom will be crucial for their widespread approval. The future of finance will be greatly influenced by how successfully central banks are able to incorporate digital currencies into current systems while working towards these goals.

Final Thoughts

Central bank digital currencies signify a major change in how money is considered and utilized. They have the ability to improve payment systems, bring in new monetary strategies, and expand the reach of financial services. Nonetheless, they present intricate hurdles, including ensuring the technical setup is secure, addressing privacy issues, and upholding trust with users. The equilibrium between central supervision and the decentralized principles that are highly esteemed in financial technology will probably play a key role in determining the adoption of CBDCs. Continuing to test and improve digital currency frameworks in countries is essential in order to gain insights from different methods. The impact of CBDCs on the financial landscape will likely change whether they reshape commercial banking or simply exist alongside traditional money forms.

In the upcoming chapter, we will shift our attention to regulation in the fintech industry. Keeping a balance between innovation and consumer protection becomes increasingly urgent with the rapid expansion of new financial technologies. We will examine how various regions handle fintech regulation, important areas requiring supervision, and the necessity of finding a balance between innovation and risk for a stable financial future.

Chapter 7

REGULATION IN FINTECH

As we examine CBDCs and their influence on finance, it is clear that fintech is transforming the financial landscape. All these advancements – AI-driven marketplaces, open banking, digital currencies – are transforming not only how individuals access financial services but also the fundamental essence of money itself. However, despite all this speed, one aspect remains constant: control. Monitoring an industry as dynamic and broad as fintech is essential to keep innovation within sight of the stability and security that individuals and businesses depend on.

This chapter will cover the regulatory landscape around fintech and the challenges and hurdles that come with running a fast-paced industry. Let's start by examining important elements of regulation, including consumer protection and equitable competition. Subsequently, we will examine them alongside actual case studies, including the US Consumer Financial Protection Bureau (CFPB) and the General Data Protection Regulation (GDPR) from the European Union. In these discussions, we will uncover how regulatory bodies are crucial in promoting the safe and equitable growth of fintech.

7.1 Key Areas of Regulation

As financial technology continues to expand, so do the responsibilities of regulatory bodies. Three main regulatory areas have emerged as focal points: consumer protection, financial system stability, and maintaining competition. Each of these areas addresses distinct concerns, yet together, they create a foundation that helps keep fintech companies accountable while allowing consumers to benefit from innovation.

Regulatory frameworks that address these areas act as a framework through which authorities can monitor fintech companies while ensuring they uphold ethical standards, financial integrity, and consumer rights. In an environment driven by rapid innovation and competition, these regulatory areas are critical. Without them, the growth of fintech could expose consumers and institutions to new risks, threatening trust in financial services.

7.1.1 Consumer Protection, Ensuring Stability in the Financial System, and Maintaining Competition

Consumer protection is central to fintech regulation. As applications emerge that enable users to handle loans, savings, investments, and intricate financial planning on their devices, regulators encounter the urgent challenge of making sure users comprehend what they are consenting to when utilizing fintech platforms. In addition to offering financial services, numerous fintech apps suggest or even counsel consumers, introducing an extra layer of accountability. Rules in this domain emphasize openness, responsible advertising, and equitable treatment of consumers, especially concerning charges, data confidentiality, and safety.

For instance, fintech applications providing investment guidance need to comply with regulations akin to those governing conventional investment companies. They should reveal risks, refrain from misleading practices, and function with an equal degree of responsibility. Likewise, lending applications are anticipated to maintain equitable lending practices, clearly communicate interest rates, and safeguard users from exploitative lending tactics that might result in debt entanglements.

Next, we consider the stability of the financial system, an essential regulatory emphasis that guarantees fintech firms do not create systemic risks. As fintech platforms optimize payments, loans, and investments, they frequently function beyond the conventional banking framework. Although this may enhance the accessibility of financial services, it may also create additional vulnerabilities. If not properly regulated, some fintech activities, like providing high-risk loans or participating in unmonitored lending, might jeopardize financial stability. Regulatory agencies intervene to reduce these risks by imposing standards that oversee the risk exposure of fintech companies, their lending behaviors, and their responsibilities to users.

Maintaining stability requires regulators to monitor the operations, data handling, and customer interactions of fintech companies. If a significant fintech firm faces a security breach or financial collapse, the repercussions could spread throughout the financial system. Consequently, regulators implement standards to guarantee that fintech platforms follow robust data protection measures and can withstand financial disturbances. In addition, these regulations aim to stop fintech firms from engaging in excessive risks that might jeopardize the stability of the entire financial ecosystem.

Lastly, maintaining competition within the fintech space is essential for fostering innovation and preventing monopolistic behavior. As fintech attracts both startup disruptors and established giants, regulatory bodies work to ensure fair play in the market. When larger corporations acquire smaller fintech firms or when fintech platforms consolidate services, the risk of monopolistic control grows. To address this, regulators set antitrust standards that keep the market accessible for new entrants, ensuring consumers continue to enjoy a diverse range of financial options.

For consumers, fair competition means access to better choices, affordable services, and more innovation. For the fintech sector, it means that companies are encouraged to develop unique offerings without the fear of being crowded out by larger entities. In other words, by safeguarding competition, regulatory bodies also drive innovation and improve service standards across the sector.

7.1.2 The Role of the CFPB in the U.S. and the Impact of GDPR in the EU

The US Consumer Financial Protection Bureau (CFPB) is one of the most famous examples of an agency that aims to protect financial consumers. In the five years since its post-crash 2008 formation, the CFPB has set high standards of transparency, fairness and accountability, particularly in the area of lending and collection. It is important to regulate fintech companies, allowing consumers to borrow money, credit, and digitally pay in order to make sure that these companies are not working in fraudulent or malicious ways. The CFPB's activities influence all aspects, from the way a fintech platform reveals fees to the protections it implements for user information.

The CFPB's responsibilities extend beyond just observing fintech firms; it also proactively establishes and upholds regulations that guarantee consumers have representation in the financial landscape. By utilizing resources such as complaint portals and consumer education tools, the CFPB enables individuals to make knowledgeable choices regarding their finances. For instance, the agency frequently subjects fintech firms to the same criteria as conventional banks, guaranteeing that consumer protection regulations are consistently enforced in both digital and physical environments. By establishing standards for transparency and fairness, the CFPB promotes a fintech landscape that is accessible, reliable, and focused on consumers.

The European Union's new General Data Protection Regulation (GDPR) has also provided an excellent model for data privacy and transparency. GDPR also mandates that EU fintech operators protect and share personal data responsibly and openly with consumers in order for them to take ownership of their data. This can include making users agree to the data collection at a minimum and data governance that's GDPR compliant for fintech companies. It obligated fintech companies to safeguard data and privacy and served as a global example for other nations as many began to make similar privacy laws in order to safeguard citizens.

But most important of all is the GDPR data portability rule, which will allow the consumer to move and access their data from one platform to another. This law allows consumers to have their data on them no matter where they go, so your data is always open, and the companies can't control your data. Compliance with GDPR is not only about the law for fintech businesses — it is also about an ecosystem that can guard, track and let users take ownership of their data. You can also be fined, which has been proven numerous times in recent years by large amounts of money slapped on the wrist by companies for GDPR.

Agencies such as the CFPB and laws such as GDPR are shaping fintech by imposing accountability and justice. They empower consumers and protect the industry through regulations regulating the business of fintech companies. We'll see, later in this chapter, how other regions are working with regulation to accomplish the same ends on a global level.

7.2 The Regulation of Fintech on a Global Scale

The worldwide expansion of fintech offers both opportunities and challenges, with regulation playing an essential role in determining how these innovations function internationally. As each region adopts its own strategy for addressing the challenges and opportunities associated with fintech, the regulatory landscape differs significantly, showcasing varying economic priorities, risk appetites, and perspectives on data privacy. For fintech firms aiming to grow globally, grasping these regulatory intricacies is crucial for achievement.

In this part, we will investigate the various methods of fintech regulation in the U.S., EU, and Asia and analyze how regulatory sandboxes have emerged as a vital mechanism for fostering innovation while safeguarding consumers.

7.2.1 Comparing Regulatory Frameworks in the U.S., EU, and Asia

There are fintech regulations across all three main markets — US, EU and Asia — depending on economics and culture. They are the policies governing the operations of fintech businesses everywhere, not just their global expansion plans.

U.S. regulation of fintech is detailed because the United States is federal. Different organizations run different parts of fintech. Securities are enforced by the Securities and Exchange Commission (SEC), national banks by the Office of the Comptroller of the Currency (OCC), and consumers are enforced by the Consumer Financial Protection Bureau (CFPB). Not only that, but every state has its own rules for digital lending and payments. It's this multifaceted regulatory jungle that provides fintech companies with such a massive market and one that demands such a large sum of money to remain compliant, especially if they are operating on a national scale.

Federal programs such as the OCC's 'fintech charter' seek to simplify this procedure by providing fintech firms with restricted banking privileges, enabling them to function across various states without needing distinct state licenses. Nonetheless, the fintech charter has encountered legal obstacles, illustrating the conflict between state and federal regulators regarding jurisdiction. Some consider the charter a tool for fostering innovation and improving financial inclusion, whereas others worry it may weaken consumer protections at the state level.

The EU, on the other hand, has had a coordinated regulatory system with universal standards for all its members. One of the biggest regulations in the world is the General Data Protection Regulation (GDPR), which sets high standards for data privacy based on what personal information companies are allowed to collect, process, and store. GDPR has hit fintech startups all over the world because every company dealing with EU citizens needs to be compliant. Furthermore, the EU's Updated Payment Services Directive (PSD2) requires banks to share their data with third-party providers upon user approval, thereby facilitating open banking. This has sparked a surge of creativity in payment systems, loan services, and budgeting applications, as fintech companies can now utilize bank information to create tailored financial offerings.

The EU's cohesive strategy streamlines adherence for fintech firms by offering one set of regulations across 27 nations. Nonetheless, it also sets elevated benchmarks for privacy and security, which may be difficult for smaller companies. The EU's emphasis on transparency and consumer rights corresponds with its wider dedication to data protection and market stability, offering a consistent basis for fintech firms that value user privacy.

In Asia, regulations for fintech greatly differ, showcasing the region's diversity. Nations such as Singapore and Hong Kong have established themselves as fintech centers by developing transparent, innovation-supportive regulatory structures. For instance, Singapore's Monetary

Authority of Singapore (MAS) has implemented a progressive strategy, providing regulatory transparency, financial benefits, and resources to draw fintech companies. The MAS promotes innovation via initiatives such as Project Ubin, which investigates the application of blockchain technology for interbank transactions. This encouraging atmosphere has turned Singapore into a favored location for fintech firms aiming to grow in Asia.

Hong Kong also provides a supportive regulatory framework aimed at promoting growth in digital payments, asset management, and insurance technology. The Hong Kong Monetary Authority (HKMA) established a 'Fintech Supervisory Sandbox' that allows firms to test innovative products prior to receiving ultimate regulatory approval, provided they meet specific risk management criteria.

However, China has been more radical in recent years. The Chinese People's Bank of China (PBOC) has tightly enforced rules on online payment and internet banking, clamping down on private fintech startups and tightening state control of the financial industry. By releasing the digital yuan, a central bank electronic money, China signaled that it would remain the economy's ruler. Although this method limits certain types of private-sector innovation, it simultaneously guarantees that fintech advancements are in line with the government's wider economic objectives.

This collection of regulatory methods necessitates that fintech companies customize their strategies for every market. In areas with favorable regulatory conditions, businesses might concentrate on swift product innovation and market growth. In more stringent jurisdictions, they need to manage compliance with greater care, making sure that their activities conform to local regulations and government goals.

7.2.2   The Importance of Regulatory Sandboxes in Testing New Fintech Products

Regulatory sandboxes are an established part of the fintech regulatory ecosystem where fintech companies test new services and products under the supervision of regulators. The sandboxes give companies the chance to try things out without breaking the rules and juggling innovation with consumer protection.

For fintech companies, sandboxes offer a crucial chance to interact with regulators early on in the development phase, obtaining insights into compliance mandates and tackling possible problems before a product launches. This is especially advantageous for emerging fintech companies that might not have the means to manage intricate regulatory environments. By engaging in a sandbox, they can evaluate their products with actual customers within set boundaries, gaining insights from feedback and improving their offerings to comply with regulatory requirements.

Nations globally have adopted the sandbox model, each customizing their strategy to align with local needs. In the UK, in 2016, the Financial Conduct Authority (FCA) established one of the first regulatory sandboxes anywhere in the world where businesses could trial products on actual users under specified guidelines. The FCA's sandbox is an innovation center that many are keen to praise as a place where companies get products out the door faster. Through its institutionalized test facility, the FCA has given fintech companies access to regulatory data and customer opinions for product quality and consumer protection.

Singapore has a very successful sandbox system, too. The Monetary Authority of Singapore (MAS) developed its sandbox program to push fintech companies to develop new products that could otherwise be blocked by the regulator. The MAS has designed its sandbox around fintech use cases from digital payments, blockchain and insurtech. Singapore's sandbox environment serves as a perfect testing platform for businesses aiming to expand throughout Asia, and it has contributed to making Singapore a prominent fintech center.

Australia has implemented a flexible sandbox model, permitting companies to trial products for as long as 24 months with a maximum of 100 clients without requiring a complete financial services license. This prolonged period allows firms to collect more substantial data on product efficacy, enabling them to enhance their products based on consumer insights and regulatory feedback. Australia's sandbox has played a key role in assisting early-stage fintech companies, creating a link between ideas and market-ready offerings.

In Hong Kong, the Hong Kong Monetary Authority (HKMA) operates a sandbox where a whole host of fintech activities — digital payments, wealth management, etc. The HKMA's sandbox provides an open-ended testing laboratory for startups to launch products that comply with Hong Kong's regulatory requirements. Hong Kong's strategy is distinctive for its focus on risk management, mandating businesses to show appropriate precautions prior to joining the sandbox.

For regulators, sandboxes provide a distinct chance to observe new developments and evaluate possible risks prior to the complete launch of products. Sandboxes enable regulators to engage directly with fintech firms, obtaining knowledge about innovative technologies and business models. This forward-thinking strategy allows regulators to remain ahead of industry changes, ensuring they can address new risks and safeguard consumers efficiently.

Sandboxes promote cooperation between fintech firms and regulators, cultivating an environment of openness and shared understanding. Collaborating in the sandbox enables companies and regulators to detect potential compliance issues early, minimizing the likelihood of enforcement actions in the future. This joint strategy is advantageous for both sides, assisting businesses in launching compliant products more quickly while allowing regulators to create a better-informed regulatory system.

The sandbox model is becoming increasingly popular worldwide, and as additional countries embrace this strategy, it contributes to establishing a more stable and predictable atmosphere for fintech innovation. Although sandboxes do not resolve all regulatory issues, they serve as an important mechanism for managing innovation and risk, ensuring that new fintech offerings undergo comprehensive and responsible testing.

Regulatory sandboxes provide a practical approach to addressing the difficulties of fintech regulation. Sandboxes create a regulated setting for experimentation, enabling fintech companies to innovate safely and responsibly, empowering them to launch new products to market with increased confidence. Simultaneously, sandboxes provide regulators with important insights into new trends, allowing them to create more efficient and flexible regulatory frameworks. As we will examine in the subsequent section, this delicate balance—promoting innovation while controlling risk—is crucial to the future of fintech oversight.

7.3   Striking a Balance Between Innovation and Risk

As fintech evolves finance, regulators must support growth while protecting the industry and its users from possible risks. This juggling act is particularly difficult due to the swift development of fintech, as new tools, products, and services constantly challenge the limits of conventional finance. Discovering the appropriate balance between regulatory oversight and the freedom to innovate involves more than simply implementing rules; it requires establishing a framework that promotes advancement while ensuring financial stability remains secure.

Global regulators are becoming more aware that an excessively strict approach may hinder innovation, restricting the advantages that fintech offers to both companies and customers. If not adequately managed, then users could be vulnerable to threats, from data theft to money laundering. The purpose of the regulation should be to develop a system where fintech companies are able to develop responsibly and identify risks that may exist before they enter the financial system as a whole.

7.3.1   How Regulations Can Promote Growth While Also Managing Risks

Efficient regulation doesn't need to hinder innovation. When carefully crafted, regulations can offer fintech companies a definitive framework, assisting them in creating products that are both compliant and advantageous. This transparency not only diminishes legal ambiguity but also enhances consumer confidence since individuals are more inclined to embrace new financial technologies when they believe their data and finances are protected.

One method for attaining this equilibrium is principles-based regulation, which establishes general guidelines instead of detailed rules. This enables businesses to adjust and innovate within a versatile regulatory structure while upholding responsibility for core principles such as consumer protection and financial stability. Regulation based on principles allows fintech companies to seek innovative solutions while still ensuring crucial protections. The Financial Conduct Authority (FCA) in the UK, for instance, highlights this strategy, seeking to promote innovation while making certain that companies operate in consumers' best interests.

Another essential strategy is regulatory collaboration. Engaging directly with fintech companies allows regulators to better comprehend new technologies and the associated risks they may pose. In exchange, businesses acquire an understanding of compliance requirements, which can influence product development from the beginning. Regulatory sandboxes, as mentioned, are essential in this context, enabling fintech companies to test innovative products in supervised settings. This partnership is advantageous for both sides: regulators remain updated on market developments, and fintech firms receive insights that assist them in improving and securing their services.

Data privacy and cybersecurity hold equal importance in sustaining this equilibrium. As fintech firms gather and handle significant volumes of personal data, regulations such as GDPR in the EU establish a minimum for privacy standards, making companies responsible for protecting user data. Although these regulations may pose difficulties for smaller businesses, they ultimately foster consumer trust and establish a basis for secure, sustainable development.

A measured approach to **risk management** is equally important. Instead of attempting to eliminate all risk—a nearly impossible goal in such a dynamic field—regulations can focus on identifying and mitigating key risks, such as those associated with digital payments, lending, and investment platforms. By enforcing transparent practices and requiring that companies maintain rigorous security measures, regulators can help minimize risks without overly constraining innovation.

Regulations serve as both guardrails and guideposts, helping fintech firms grow with purpose. The aim isn't to control every move but to create an environment where innovation thrives safely and responsibly. A balanced approach to fintech regulation can provide clarity, protect consumers, and support a financial ecosystem that's both dynamic and secure. This alignment of growth and stability will be key as fintech continues to redefine how we interact with money and financial services.

Final Thoughts

This chapter emphasizes that regulation is vital for the sustainable growth of fintech. Regulations serve more than just establishing limits—they safeguard consumers, ensure stability in financial systems, and promote equitable competition. Nevertheless, regulation in fintech is not fixed; it needs to develop in tandem with the innovations it governs. Finding the proper equilibrium between promoting growth and maintaining security is crucial for creating a fintech ecosystem that benefits all stakeholders.

Careful regulation offers the framework necessary for fintech to innovatively reshape financial services in a responsible manner. Efforts such as regulatory sandboxes and principles-driven frameworks are demonstrating that growth and safety can coexist effectively. In the future, fintech companies and regulators will need to keep adjusting this balance to ensure that new technologies complement the financial system in the best possible ways.

In the following chapters we will see the future of fintech and what's driving this like decentralized finance, AI, and the emergence of digital currencies. We will explore the technologies that fuel these changes—blockchain, IoT, and the future-opening promise of quantum computing. Looking forward, we will examine the skills and tactics necessary to succeed in an industry poised for even more significant change. The outlook for fintech is highly promising, and those ready to adjust will spearhead the forthcoming wave of financial advancements.

Chapter 8

THE FUTURE OF FINTECH

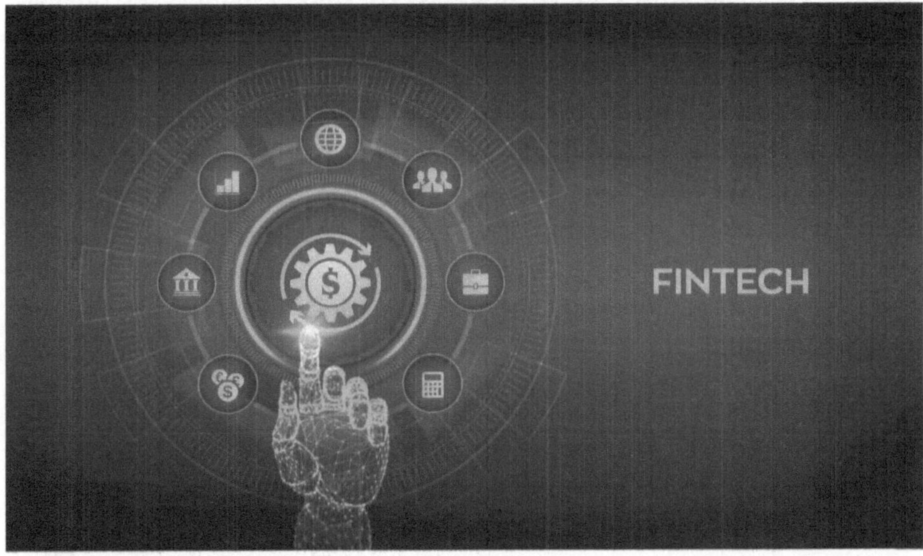

Fintech, as we've seen, needs to be regulated to ensure innovation, consumer protection, and stability. These regulations matter because fintech is winging its way out of existence. It's an industry in which the pace of technology innovation is rapidly picking up, and the industry phase ahead will be more massive than ever. DeFi, CBDCs and artificial intelligence (AI) represent a new wave of innovation that will transform the way we think about money.

In this chapter, we will talk about Fintech developments like DeFi platforms, CBDCs, and the increasing significance of AI. We'll see how these trends will remake the financial services system into something open and affordable. Future discussions will be about the ways in which enabling technologies – blockchain, IoT, quantum computing, etc. – enable this transformation. We will then finish talking about what it takes for people to be successful in this fast-growing sector and how businesses can act to stay ahead of things.

8.1.1 Expansion in DeFi, More CBDCs, and AI Fueling the New Wave of Innovation

This is the new dawn of Fintech driven by developments like DeFi, CBDCs, and artificial intelligence (AI). All these technologies are making finance a new, more open-ended entity, and together, they're making the financial industry more open. DeFi is probably the most radical transformation we've ever experienced. DeFi applications, all based on blockchain, enable individuals to lend, borrow, trade and even earn interest without banks. DeFi instead deploys 'smart contracts' that automatically trigger transactions based on certain conditions. DeFi's strength lies in being open and agile; users have complete ownership of their assets and can easily interact with other users on the platform. DeFi began primarily in crypto circles but is now emerging as an important alternative to the financial services industry for a broader audience.

Central banks around the globe are working on creating their own digital currencies on a different front. These Central Bank Digital Currencies are essentially electronic adaptations of official currencies intended to expedite and enhance the security of transactions. Unlike cryptocurrencies, they have the support of governments, meaning individuals can depend on them in the same way they trust traditional currency. Nations such as China have started implementing digital currencies in practical situations, while the European Union and the U.S. are exploring their potential applications. For numerous individuals, particularly those lacking convenient bank services, CBDCs may provide a safe method to engage in the online economy.

Artificial intelligence is enhancing this transition by increasing the level of personalization and intelligence in finance. AI enables financial institutions to rapidly analyze vast quantities of data, recognizing patterns and trends that assist in providing improved services. AI is able to identify possible fraud, foresee changes in the market, and offer customer assistance through chatbots that can answer inquiries instantly, 24/7. Fintech is progressing towards a future where financial services are not only more accessible but also more personalized by combining AI with DeFi and CBDCs.

Together, DeFi, CBDCs, and AI are creating new possibilities, giving people more choices, control, and efficiency in managing their finances. This trio of technologies is setting the stage for the next wave of fintech, one where users are at the center.

8.1.2 Fintech's Influence on Traditional Financial Services: Making Financial Services More Accessible

One major impact of fintech is the increased accessibility of financial services for all individuals. Technology is dismantling old obstacles, making previously unattainable opportunities accessible to individuals and small companies.

For instance, consider lending. In the past, traditional loans needed a long credit history, but now, many fintech platforms use advanced algorithms to consider more factors in applications. This change allows individuals without a credit history, such as young adults or those in developing countries, to have a chance to get credit. Small enterprises are also reaping the rewards of quicker, more straightforward loan access, which can aid in their expansion without the obstacles of conventional banking criteria.

Fintech is altering how individuals handle their daily financial matters. Mobile banking apps, budgeting tools, and investment platforms enable users to manage finances and investments on their smartphones. Mobile wallets are filling the void in areas where banks are scarce, allowing individuals to digitally save and use their money. By using only a phone, individuals have the ability to purchase necessary items, transfer money to their relatives, and participate in various transactions that they might otherwise overlook.

Investing has become much easier to access in recent times. People can begin investing with small amounts thanks to platforms offering fractional shares, and they can receive personalized advice at an affordable cost through robo-advisors. These instruments create chances for individuals to build wealth who may have previously believed that investing was unattainable.

Fintech is enabling a greater number of individuals to manage their financial well-being by expanding these services to be more accessible. Traditional banks are observing that Fintech is enabling a greater number of individuals to control their financial situation by expanding the availability of services. Traditional banks are also recognizing this shift. Many people are adopting similar technologies and partnering with fintech firms to stay relevant in this rapidly changing landscape. In this modern age, financial tools are no longer limited to a select few; they are becoming common for all.

8.2   The Role of New Technologies in the Future

It is evident that in the future, newer technologies will revolutionize finance in ways we are only starting to envision. Certain innovations, such as blockchain and AI, are already impacting the world, while others, like quantum computing, are still establishing themselves. However, every single one has significant possibilities for how we will handle finances, protect our information, and carry out daily transactions in the future.

Blockchain, AI, IoT, and quantum computing offer unique advantages individually. Collectively, they are shaping a future where finance is quicker, more intelligent, and highly integrated. Let's dive deeper into the capacities of each of these technologies.

8.2.1   The Influence of Blockchain, AI, IoT, and Quantum Computing

Although commonly associated with cryptocurrencies, blockchain serves purposes beyond solely digital money. Blockchain is simply a digital record-keeping system in which transactions can be recorded securely and openly. What's different is that it doesn't rely on a central source of information, like a bank, to validate transactions. Conversely, every transaction is confirmed and documented on a network of computers, greatly reducing the chance of changes after being added. This configuration provides a level of security and assurance that traditional systems may find difficult to offer.

This presents various opportunities in the field of finance. Imagine a situation where international transactions are completed immediately, with low fees, and without involving numerous intermediaries. Blockchain can improve the visibility of supply chains. One possible use of blockchain is to track each step of a product's journey from maker to vendor, guaranteeing visibility and authentication at every point. This has the potential to greatly decrease fraud, improve transparency, and build trust among all individuals involved. Predictions suggest that as blockchain technology is adopted across various sectors, its impact on the financial industry will grow, leading to a more efficient and trustworthy financial landscape.

Artificial intelligence (AI) is majorly influencing finance, and its effects are already evident. Think about the banking applications that alert you of uncommon transactions according to your spending routines or the digital helpers that can respond to inquiries about your account around the clock. This is AI in motion—examining large quantities of data, identifying patterns, and creating a more personalized financial experience. AI excels in processing data on a scale and speed that surpasses human capabilities. Within moments, it is capable of examining user actions, detecting possible fraud, forecasting patterns, and assisting financial organizations in promptly assisting their clients.

AI can assist individuals in making intelligent financial choices. Picture getting personalized suggestions for managing finances, investing, or reducing debt that is tailored to your individual financial circumstances. Often, AI functions as a financial advisor prepared to assist in understanding your finances. Progress in artificial intelligence will lead to more customized financial choices based on data, changing how we handle money matters.

While it may seem futuristic, the Internet of Things (IoT) is already present, linking regular devices to the Internet in ways that provide tangible benefits. Smartphones, smartwatches, and connected cars are included in this network and are improving our lives by increasing connectivity. IoT involves allowing regular objects to interact by sharing data with each other and with humans. This connection is integrating finance into more parts of our everyday lives, sometimes without our awareness.

Practically speaking, IoT might involve a smartwatch reminding you about a bill due or a car that pays tolls and parking fees automatically. IoT can be used by businesses to monitor shipments live and guarantee that products arrive at their destination as planned. With the increasing number of devices connecting to the internet, the impact of IoT is expected to expand, possibly transforming financial transactions into a seamless, automated process. This convenience could change our expectations, transforming finance from a solitary task to a seamless part of everyday life.

Quantum computing may not be very well known, but it is also one of the most thrilling technologies. Unlike classical computers, which use binary bits to process data, quantum computers utilize qubits that can hold multiple states simultaneously. This indicates that quantum computers can solve highly intricate problems much quicker than our current machines. In the field of finance, quantum computing may open up new opportunities, particularly in sectors that involve extensive data analysis, such as encryption, risk assessment, and market forecasting.

Imagine having the ability to predict changes in the market or identify security risks instantly. Quantum computing might bring us much closer to achieving that vision. Despite being in its initial phase, this technology has the potential to significantly impact finance by providing financial institutions with solutions for currently unattainable challenges. As quantum technology advances, it could lead to unprecedented levels of financial security and analysis.

Every one of these technologies, including blockchain, AI, IoT, and quantum computing, possesses distinct advantages, and together they are influencing the future of finance. Their impact is amplified when they are combined. These advancements are not just current fads; they are developing resources that can help simplify, enhance, and add value to money management. As these advancements progress, they will create a financial landscape in which transactions are quicker, decisions are better informed, and our interactions with money are smoother than before.

8.3   Preparing for the Future

Staying current in the rapidly evolving fintech landscape is a considerable challenge. Having technical knowledge alone is not enough to remain important - flexibility, prioritizing customer satisfaction, and willingness to embrace new perspectives are also essential. This entails individuals developing the necessary skills to meet the changing requirements of fintech. For businesses, it's important to establish a flexible and forward-thinking atmosphere. Here is how both parties can prepare for the future.

8.3.1 The Skills People Will Need to Thrive in Fintech

As fintech expands, the required skills are changing, combining technical knowledge with a solid understanding of finance and user requirements. Here is an overview of the combination of abilities that are becoming crucial in this industry.

To begin with, let's discuss technical abilities. The use of data analysis is increasingly becoming a fundamental aspect of fintech. Data is crucial for numerous fintech applications, ranging from customer insights to fraud detection. Having a strong grasp of working with data, whether it is analyzing, interpreting trends, or using data for informed decisions, provides a significant benefit. Having knowledge of programming languages such as Python, SQL, or R can help you grasp the flow of data and influence financial choices. Learning the fundamentals of blockchain and AI can distinguish you, especially as more platforms incorporate these technologies. Gaining knowledge of smart contract functionality or the fundamentals of machine learning algorithms is not only beneficial but also useful for interacting with these systems in practical scenarios.

However, only possessing technical skills is not enough. The fintech sector values individuals who excel at problem-solving and innovative thinking. What is the reason? Since fintech focuses on simplifying, speeding up, and enhancing the user experience of financial procedures. Consider this: every service you offer, or solution you create must satisfy the requirements of actual individuals. Taking a user-centered approach, identifying areas of frustration, and creating intuitive solutions can have a significant impact. Individuals who possess the ability to create or enhance user experiences will continue to be sought after as they assist in connecting intricate technology with everyday individuals.

Being adaptable is essential in today's world. Fintech is always evolving. Rules change, advancements in technology occur, and fresh customer demands appear on a regular basis. Those who excel in fintech view change as a chance to develop rather than a disturbance. Staying open to ongoing learning, whether by mastering a new tool, exploring a different aspect of fintech, or staying updated on current trends, is essential for maintaining flexibility and preparedness for the future. Adaptability is a competency and an attitude that enables you to progress despite shifts in the industry.

Ultimately, possessing a strong grasp of financial concepts is highly beneficial. Understanding the fundamentals of borrowing, transactions, financial growth, and controlling uncertainties can assist in connecting technology with practical financial situations. Having both technological and financial expertise enables you to identify potential advantages, comprehend the obstacles customers encounter, and provide better-informed input on projects. In essence, individuals who understand both technology and finance add a special value to any group, contributing to the development of fintech products that are both innovative and practical.

8.3.2 How Organizations Can Adapt and Stay Competitive

Remaining competitive in the fintech industry for organizations involves fostering a culture that values innovation and adapts to market demands. Businesses that quickly adjust to changes and cultivate a team prepared for those changes will succeed in this rapidly evolving industry. Here are the ways for organizations to stay current:

Investing in their employees is a major way for a company to get ready for the future. Creating a talented and flexible team requires continuous dedication, not just a one-time endeavor. Providing ongoing learning opportunities such as training programs, new tool access, and trend workshops helps teams stay informed and capable of facing new challenges. Encouraging employees to develop both their technical skills and their knowledge of user experience not only helps them but also strengthens the organization. A team that has current skills and knowledge is more ready to handle new solutions, adjust to evolving technologies, and address difficult issues as they come up.

Besides training, establishing an innovative culture is crucial. In the world of financial technology, new concepts are vital for progress. Businesses that promote innovation test out new technologies, and embrace trial and error tend to be at the forefront. This may involve scheduling frequent idea-generation meetings, forming small teams with varied expertise to investigate innovative concepts, or offering a platform for staff to display their own initiatives. When companies consistently encourage innovation, they are more likely to maintain a competitive edge in their industry.

Collaboration is also a crucial element. The success of fintech relies on collaborations, whether a startup collaborates with a bank, a tech company partners with a financial institution, or different sectors unite to provide innovative services. Working together provides new opportunities for companies to exchange information, create more thorough answers, and expand their reach to a larger group of people. Organizations that are receptive to such collaborations and ready to gain knowledge from others can create more robust, flexible products. When teams with diverse backgrounds and skills collaborate, they can often develop solutions that cater to a wider array of needs than they could individually.

Remaining focused on the customer is equally important. Ultimately, the aim of fintech is to simplify and enhance access to finance for individuals. Businesses that prioritize their customers—by consistently seeking feedback, testing innovations with clients, and adjusting their products based on real-world usage—are more apt to thrive. The fintech companies that are at the forefront are those that create solutions tailored to their users' lives, not just products. Taking into account customer input and implementing adjustments, like enhancing the user interface or integrating security measures, can result in a notable difference.

Ultimately, embracing adaptability in tactics allows businesses to respond to unexpected alterations, like changes in laws, emerging market needs, or advancements in technology. Fintech firms must be prepared to adapt swiftly and make changes as required. This could involve going back to the main products of the company, adjusting a product to fulfill a new need, or releasing a new version with updated information. Having a flexible approach allows companies to stay agile and effectively deal with any challenges or opportunities that arise.

In the realm of fintech, individuals and organizations are adapting to a constantly changing landscape. For those who are prepared to adopt a mindset focused on learning, innovation, and prioritizing customers, the future offers vast opportunities. By remaining flexible, developing relevant abilities, and concentrating on impactful resolutions, individuals and businesses cannot just survive but flourish in this ever-changing field.

Final Thoughts

Fintech is constantly changing as DeFi, CBDCs, and AI transform the financial industry. These advancements are shifting finance towards a future that is more easily accessible, efficient and focused on the user. Blockchain, AI, IoT, and quantum computing all possess distinct advantages, ranging from secure transactions to data-driven insights, offering a financial landscape that is quicker and more intelligent.

In order to succeed in this field, people must mix technical expertise with a thorough comprehension of user requirements, while organizations should focus on flexibility, ongoing education, and a work environment that encourages creativity. Organizations that prioritize their employees form collaborations and emphasize customer experience will be in a strong position to take the lead. Fintech's growth continues to emphasize a future of easier money management, better-informed decisions, and accessible financial tools for all.

Chapter 9

BUILDING A CAREER IN FINTECH

We have assessed the technologies, trends, and obstacles that are shaping the future of FinTech. The rise of AI and DeFi, along with ongoing digital progress in multiple industries, indicates that FinTech is not just changing but also shifting towards a fundamentally new direction. With the growing scope of these technologies, there is an increasing need for proficient professionals to implement them.

> **Fun Fact:**
>
> *The global fintech market is expected to reach $556 billion by 2030, and startup funding is growing rapidly, especially in sectors like digital wallets and DeFi.*

In this part, we will focus on the essential components required to build a successful career in this rapidly evolving industry. We will talk about the essential technical and financial skills needed for success, examine the emerging job roles in the FinTech sector, and offer guidance for achieving long-lasting success. We will also look into the essential actions required to start a FinTech business for individuals with an entrepreneurial approach, emphasizing the advice, tactics, and tools needed to launch your concepts successfully. Whether you are interested in joining a FinTech company or launching your own venture, this chapter provides useful advice for achieving success in the FinTech sector.

9.1   Skills for a Successful Career in FinTech

FinTech is a field in which creativity intersects with real-world implementation, necessitating a blend of technical understanding, financial acumen, and flexibility to achieve success. It's more than just having good tech skills or knowing financial terms - it's about combining them to find practical solutions for real-life problems. Having the correct blend of skills is essential, whether you are creating a payment app, analyzing data for fraud detection, or overseeing compliance.

In this part, we will examine the abilities that can distinguish you, the subjects worth becoming proficient in, and how to prepare for advancement in this quickly evolving field.

9.1.1   Key Technical and Financial Skills to Focus On

Achieving success in FinTech requires a combination of technical and financial expertise. When professionals successfully integrate these two areas, they can excel in a field that prioritizes innovation and practicality.

1.   Technical Skills: The Foundation for Innovation

Having a strong foundation in technology is key in FinTech, as expertise in the appropriate technical resources can provide opportunities throughout the field. Here are the main areas to concentrate on:

Programming Languages: Discover programming languages such as Java,. Net, Python, R, and JavaScript, commonly utilized for creating financial algorithms, data analysis tools, and web-based applications. Python excels in tasks such as data manipulation and machine learning, whereas JavaScript drives interactive features within financial platforms.

Data Analytics: FinTech is powered by data, whether it's information on customer preferences, transaction habits, or market movements. Acquiring skills in SQL to manage databases and utilizing platforms like Tableau or Power BI to visualize data can enable you to uncover practical insights.

Artificial Intelligence and Machine Learning: AI is used for a variety of tasks, such as identifying fraudulent activities and providing personalized financial tips. It is crucial to comprehend how algorithms analyze data and enhance their performance as time goes on. Exploring neural networks and predictive modeling can enhance your knowledge.

Blockchain Technology: Blockchain knowledge is growing in importance for those involved in DeFi applications or digital currencies. Concentrate on comprehending distributed ledgers, agreement mechanisms, and tools such as Solidity, which is utilized for creating smart contracts.

Cybersecurity - A Must-Have Skill in FinTech:

In a world where digital money transfers are common, having cybersecurity expertise is vital for individuals in the FinTech industry. Given the increasing incidents of online fraud, data breaches, and ransomware attacks, safeguarding sensitive financial information is of utmost importance. Understanding how to develop secure systems is not only a technical ability but also a means to gain trust and assurance in the field.

To develop skills in cybersecurity, concentrate on these essential areas:

Encryption

Gain knowledge of protecting data through encryption methods for both transmission and storage. This guarantees that confidential data remains inaccessible to unauthorized individuals, even if it is intercepted.

Ethical Hacking

Knowing the tactics of attackers can assist in identifying and addressing vulnerabilities in systems proactively, preventing exploitation. The concept of ethical hacking involves keeping ahead of possible threats.

Threat Detection and Response

Get ready with the tools and knowledge needed to detect potential attacks as they happen. Fast and efficient reactions to cyber threats can stop minor problems from escalating into significant issues.

Compliance Standards

Get acquainted with rules such as PCI DSS and GDPR. These regulations do more than just enforce laws - they also guarantee the security of systems and the protection of user privacy.

Acquiring these skills will place you in a powerful position to successfully overcome FinTech's technical obstacles. In addition to problem-solving, you will also have a crucial part in creating secure solutions that instill trust in users and stakeholders.

2. Financial Skills: The Practical Side of Innovation

In FinTech, comprehending technology is just one part of the equation. An equally crucial aspect is a deep understanding of financial fundamentals. Fundamentally, FinTech involves addressing financial obstacles with creative solutions, necessitating strong expertise in both fields.

Here's why financial knowledge is indispensable:

Understanding Financial Products

Having a comprehensive understanding of financial products like payments, loans, insurance, and wealth management is crucial for developing successful solutions. Comprehending how these services operate helps you create tools that meet specific needs and smoothly blend into everyday use.

Regulations and Compliance

Stringent rules are implemented to oversee financial systems and ensure confidence and steadiness. Understanding regulations like anti-money laundering (AML) laws and Know Your Customer (KYC) requirements allows you to develop compliant systems that ensure users feel secure with their information and funds.

Risk Management

Every financial decision comes with a level of unpredictability. Understanding how to measure and minimize credit risk, market risk, and operational risk is essential for creating secure and reliable solutions.

Customer-Centric Design

Having knowledge of financial matters allows you to understand the perspective of the customer. Designing solutions that truly meet their needs involves understanding their pain points, such as credit access, expense management, and saving for the future.

3. Combining Technical and Financial Expertise

Individuals in FinTech who possess these skills can uncover market deficiencies and devise solutions that are both technically solid and economically sustainable. A blockchain developer with knowledge of lending mechanisms can create DeFi applications with smooth user interfaces. Likewise, a data scientist who understands financial regulations can develop fraud detection systems that fulfill compliance standards.

Acquiring these skills not only improves your performance but also provides opportunities for specialized roles that demand this distinctive combination. It is not only about completing tasks but also about comprehending the reason for each skill and using that understanding to create new ideas.

9.2 FinTech Job Roles

The FinTech sector succeeds by combining advanced technology, precise analysis, and strict adherence to regulations. This combination of abilities has created a variety of specific job positions that are transforming the field of finance. These roles are not just popular but also necessitate a strong grasp of the overlap between technology and financial systems. In this part, we will concentrate on three crucial positions: data scientists, blockchain developers, and compliance officers, discussing their duties, contributions, and the specific skills needed to succeed in each role.

9.2.1 Overview of Roles Such as Data Scientists, Blockchain Developers, and Compliance Officers

Data Scientists: The Analysts Who Power FinTech Innovation

In FinTech, data scientists play a crucial role as data is the key factor that guides decision-making and creativity. Their job involves analyzing extensive datasets to find valuable information like customer actions, purchase records, or market patterns. Their capacity to assess, explain, and exhibit this data turns unprocessed information into plans that enhance products, simplify operations, and elevate user interactions.

For instance, a data scientist employed at a digital wallet firm could examine spending trends to develop predictive models that provide customized financial guidance. This might involve suggesting methods to cut costs on monthly memberships or alerting about suspicious spending to avoid fraud. Data scientists use machine learning algorithms to create systems that can improve their accuracy and effectiveness by learning and adapting over time.

The qualifications needed for this position extend beyond just technical knowledge. Although data scientists should possess strong programming abilities in Python or R, it is equally crucial for them to excel in storytelling, effectively conveying their findings to motivate actions. Their importance lies in connecting numbers to business results, making sure that data is used to improve decision-making. The need for proficient data scientists will keep increasing as FinTech firms rely more on data to maintain competitiveness.

Blockchain Developers: Architects of Decentralization

Blockchain developers build the foundation of decentralized finance, digital currency, and other innovative financial technologies. Their job involves building and keeping secure, transparent, and scalable blockchain systems. This involves the creation of smart contracts (codes that execute transactions based on conditions) and dApps, allowing users to engage directly with blockchain platforms.

Imagine a blockchain developer creating a DeFi lending platform. Their responsibility might involve guaranteeing the accuracy, effectiveness, and security of smart loan contracts. They might also enhance the platform to support large-scale transactions without compromising its security or speed. Blockchain developers need to have a strong understanding of programming languages like Solidity and Rust, as well as cryptography and distributed ledger technologies.

The significance of this position extends well beyond just the execution of technical tasks. Blockchain developers are changing the way financial services are provided, increasing accessibility and reducing dependence on traditional institutions. Their efforts in cutting out middlemen create pathways for systems that are not just effective but also welcoming, providing chances to individuals previously left out of traditional banking.

Compliance Officers: Guardians of Trust in Innovation

As FinTech pushes the limits of financial innovation, compliance officers make sure these advances adhere to legal and ethical standards. Their function is essential in upholding trust with customers, regulators, and stakeholders. They supervise compliance with regulations like GDPR,

PSD2, and AML laws, carrying out audits and establishing policies to reduce risks.

A compliance officer at a FinTech firm could collaborate extensively with product teams to guarantee that a new payment application adheres to local and global regulations. This may include evaluating the app's data collection procedures to protect customer privacy or confirming that its transaction monitoring systems are strong enough to identify potential wrongdoing. In addition to their knowledge of regulations, compliance officers must also have strong communication skills to train teams and promote an accountable culture in the organization.

The importance of this role goes far beyond simply completing technical duties. Developers in the blockchain industry are transforming the delivery of financial services by enhancing accessibility and lessening reliance on conventional institutions. Their endeavors to eliminate intermediaries pave the way for systems that are both efficient and inviting, offering opportunities to individuals who were previously excluded from conventional banking. This role's value is in its capacity to maintain a balance between innovation and responsibility. In an industry where trust is crucial, compliance officers serve as a connection between innovative concepts and operational honesty. Their efforts guarantee that FinTech firms can continue to innovate while upholding legal and ethical norms, proving to be vital to the sector.

A Dynamic and Collaborative Ecosystem

The data scientists, blockchain developers, and compliance officers are essential components of the FinTech workforce. Each person offers a distinct skill set that contributes to the common objective of developing smarter, safer, and more inclusive financial solutions. Data scientists offer the wisdom that fuels change, blockchain developers construct the framework that enables it, and compliance officers guarantee that it functions ethically.

Collaboration is essential in the thriving industry of FinTech. Success in these positions typically relies on professionals' capacity to collaborate across various teams and areas of expertise rather than working independently. An example would be a fraud detection model by a data scientist that depends on a secure system created by a blockchain developer, with input needed from a compliance officer for regulatory alignment. The interconnectedness of FinTech roles emphasizes the significance of both personal skills and collaborative work.

As the field progresses, these positions will keep changing, providing chances for professionals to advance with the new advancements they contribute to. Whether you're interested in the technical, analytical, or regulatory facets of FinTech, there is a route that enables you to make a significant contribution to one of the most revolutionary industries of our time.

The importance of this role goes far beyond simply completing technical duties. Developers in the blockchain industry are transforming the delivery of financial services by enhancing accessibility and lessening reliance on conventional institutions. Their endeavors to eliminate intermediaries pave the way for systems that are both efficient and inviting, offering opportunities to individuals who were previously excluded from conventional banking. This role's value is in its capacity to maintain a balance between innovation and responsibility. In an industry where trust is crucial, compliance officers serve as a connection between innovative concepts and operational honesty. Their efforts guarantee that FinTech firms can continue to innovate while upholding legal and ethical norms, proving to be vital to the sector.

9.3   Tips for Success

Achieving success in FinTech involves more than just having technical skills or financial acumen. It's about keeping up in an industry where change is continual, competition is strong, and prepared individuals are rewarded with opportunities. Although each career path is different, there are common tactics that can assist you in succeeding in this field. This part will be about the significance of ongoing education, the benefits of focusing on a specific area, and the importance of making connections in establishing a fulfilling career in FinTech.

Pro Tip:

Many fintech professionals land jobs through networking! Don't underestimate the power of a friendly coffee chat or attending an industry event.

9.3.1 Why Are Continuous Learning, Specializing in a Specific Area, and Networking Important?

Continuous Learning: Staying Ahead in a Competitive Industry

The field of FinTech is a center of creative ideas. The frequent emergence of new technologies, tools, and frameworks highlights the importance of staying up-to-date, as it is not just advantageous but also necessary. Ongoing learning enables professionals to stay competitive and adjust to new challenges. This is crucial in an industry where AI models, blockchain protocols, or regulatory standards could change drastically from year to year.

Think about artificial intelligence: a field where developments like GPT-powered models and enhanced neural networks are changing the way financial data is handled. Someone who became proficient in AI methods five years ago but hasn't kept up-to-date with their skills is in danger of lagging behind. Enrolling in online classes, earning certifications, and participating in self-directed learning provide chances to keep current on the latest advancements and utilize them effectively. For instance, having expertise in emerging programming languages like Solidity for blockchain or improving data visualization abilities for more effective presentations can make you more noticeable in a competitive industry.

Yet, ongoing education is not solely focused on technical abilities. It is also about comprehending the practical applications of these technologies to real-life issues. Participating in industry events, reading thought leadership articles, or becoming a member of professional communities can provide you with diverse perspectives beyond just coding or finance. By dedicating yourself to continuous learning, you guarantee that your knowledge stays current and useful.

Specializing in a Specific Area: Becoming an Expert Rather Than a Generalist

Although it may be tempting to become proficient in everything, FinTech favors individuals who specialize in specific areas. Having a specific expertise helps you differentiate yourself in a field that prioritizes accuracy and expertise. By specializing in data analytics, cybersecurity, or blockchain development, you can become known as the leading expert in your respective field.

For instance, a blockchain developer with expertise in creating efficient smart contracts is essential for teams involved in DeFi projects. Likewise, FinTech companies seeking global expansion greatly benefit from having a compliance officer who possesses a thorough knowledge of cross-border regulations. Specializing in a certain area can lead to increased demand for your expertise and more chances to take on leadership positions.

To specialize, identify areas that align with your interests and the industry's needs. Then, dive deeper into those topics through advanced courses, projects, or hands-on experience. Build a portfolio or case studies that demonstrate your expertise. Over time, your focus can open doors to niche roles or high-impact projects that generalists may not access.

Networking: Building Connections That Propel Your Career

In the field of FinTech, as well as in various other sectors, having the right connections is frequently the key to success. Networking involves more than just gathering business cards or making connections on LinkedIn; it involves developing significant relationships that can result in partnerships, guidance, or advancements. The interconnectedness of FinTech necessitates collaboration among various disciplines for many roles. Networking enables you to form the necessary connections to succeed in this environment.

Participating in conferences, attending FinTech meetups, or joining hackathons can allow you to network with peers, industry experts, and possible partners. These occasions provide an avenue not only for learning but also for demonstrating your abilities and concepts. Talking to a blockchain expert could motivate you to venture into a different field while conversing with a business owner might result in a collaboration.

Building connections is just as crucial for advancing in your career. A lot of FinTech positions are filled through referrals or recommendations. A robust network can provide you with opportunities before others, understanding of company culture, or guidance on overcoming obstacles. Establishing authentic connections demands work—providing assistance, exchanging information, and keeping contact—yet the rewards can be substantial.

The Intersection of Learning, Specialization, and Networking

Continuous learning, specialization, and networking are not separate paths—they overlap and reinforce one another. For instance, networking can introduce you to experts who inspire you to specialize, while learning ensures your expertise remains cutting-edge. Together, these strategies form a foundation for long-term success in FinTech.

To thrive in this field, approach your career as a journey of growth. Commit to learning, focus on what you do best, and invest in relationships that support and amplify your goals. In a sector that values innovation and collaboration, these habits will not only keep you relevant but also position you for sustained success.

9.4   Opportunities for Entrepreneurs

The FinTech industry offers many opportunities to individuals aspiring to innovate and create new things. Thanks to advancements like AI, blockchain, and open banking, entrepreneurs can seize opportunities in the market where traditional businesses have failed to solve issues. From improving financial inclusion to developing new investment tools, FinTech provides a fertile environment for innovative ideas to flourish. Nevertheless, in FinTech, it takes more than just a good idea to start a successful business. Entrepreneurs need to blend vision with practical implementation, mixing creativity with a solid grasp of market demands, regulations, and scalability. This section is about the process, methods, and understanding required to create a successful FinTech company.

9.4.1   Key Insights for Starting Your Own FinTech Venture

Launching a FinTech startup starts by pinpointing a valuable problem that needs to be addressed. Many thriving startups prioritize addressing issues ignored by conventional banks, like offering low-cost loans to underserved areas or developing efficient international payment platforms. Study the market extensively in order to discover your niche. Search for inefficiencies, unfulfilled customer needs, or obsolete processes that could be modernized using technology. Valuable insights commonly arise from personal experiences or in-depth investigation of consumer frustrations.

After you have a defined concept, the next move is to confirm its validity. Validating early can help avoid expensive mistakes and significantly reduce the amount of time spent on a project. Develop a basic version of your product to showcase your idea and evaluate it with a specific group of users. This procedure is not only about validating your technology but also about verifying that it addresses an actual issue. Collect input, improve your solution, and confirm demand before expanding. Having a good grasp of the regulatory environment is just as crucial. Ignoring regulatory compliance can derail even the most innovative startups within the tightly regulated FinTech environment. Study the regulations applicable to your product, whether related to data privacy, anti-money laundering obligations, or payment processing criteria. Numerous administrations provide regulatory sandboxes, which are controlled environments for startups to test their solutions and ensure compliance with legal standards. Utilizing these frameworks can ensure adherence to regulations while still allowing for creativity to flourish.

Technology is essential for any FinTech business, so it is important to have a strong and scalable tech stack. Whether you're creating a digital wallet or a blockchain-based lending platform, make sure to focus on secure and efficient systems. Work with developers who grasp the complexities of FinTech and remember the importance of cybersecurity. Trust is imperative in this sector, and safeguarding your customers' information should be a main focus from the beginning. Securing financial support is another vital aspect of the situation. Startups in the FinTech industry often need a substantial amount of money upfront to develop, license, and market their products. Present your concept to investors such as venture capitalists, angel investors, or accelerators with a focus on financial technology. Make sure you are ready to clearly explain your value proposition, market potential, and revenue model. Forming strong relationships with appropriate partners from the beginning can offer more than just funding, such as connections to useful networks and specialized knowledge.

As crucial as it is to create the right product, creating the right team is equally important. FinTech encompasses different disciplines, and a thriving startup needs a variety of skills. Create a group with a blend of technical, financial, and operational expertise. Search for individuals who have a similar outlook as you but possess different skills that can add value. A united and competent team can bring even the most ambitious ideas to fruition. Never underestimate the impact of collaborations. Teaming up with traditional institutions like banks, payment processors, or other FinTech firms can expedite growth and expand into different markets. For example, teaming up with a conventional bank could help you utilize their framework while providing an innovative, technology-based answer. Building strategic partnerships can enhance your reach and credibility, facilitating greater success in a competitive market.

Starting a FinTech startup presents difficulties but also brings satisfaction. Having a sharp focus on addressing actual issues, being dedicated to innovation, and being able to quickly adjust to technological and regulatory changes are necessary. Entrepreneurs can establish businesses that not only succeed but also change how the world engages with money by merging a clear vision with disciplined execution.

Final Thoughts

The FinTech sector goes beyond just being a hub for creativity - it serves as a space where technology and finance come together to address global issues. Both professionals and entrepreneurs have unique chances to make a difference, develop innovative solutions, and influence how we use money in the future in this industry.

In this chapter, we have examined the abilities, positions, and tactics required for success in FinTech. The opportunities are abundant but require focus, adaptability, and commitment, whether you are mastering technical and financial skills, taking on different job roles, or starting a business venture. Succeeding in this field involves understanding that it's more than just keeping up - it's about being one step ahead. By dedicating oneself to ongoing learning, honing your expertise, and establishing valuable connections, you can establish a rewarding and prosperous career in FinTech.

You have the tools in your possession. The chances are there for you to take advantage of. It is now time to take action.

AFTERWORD

As we wrap up this exploration into the world of FinTech, it is clear that it is more than just a trend. It is a technological-driven movement that is driven by innovation, aiming to enhance accessibility, security, and inclusivity in financial services. Ever since credit cards and ATMs. were introduced, FinTech has continuously pushed limits with advancements such as blockchain and AI, altering our perceptions of what could be accomplished.

Nevertheless, this is just the beginning. The evolution of FinTech will depend on people who dare to think creatively, challenge the status quo, and combine new ideas with practical applications. If you wish to join this movement in a professional capacity, as a business owner, or simply as an informed individual, this book provides a solid starting point. The true value and benefits come from putting these teachings into practice to address actual challenges in the real world. Keep in mind that the tale of FinTech is still evolving. Every fresh discovery, each creative new company, and the entire team working quietly in the background are all playing a part in shaping this developing story. Now, it's up to you to join in. Utilize the tools, strategies, and knowledge you have acquired to create your journey ahead. The future of FinTech should not only be observed but also actively shaped.

I appreciate you taking the time to explore the fintech industry with me. I sincerely trust that the wisdom and tactics presented in this book have prompted fresh thoughts, simplified difficult ideas, or even encouraged you to venture into this ever-changing field. If you need personalized assistance with starting a payment gateway, launching a digital wallet, exploring cryptocurrency opportunities, or entering the fintech industry, I'd be glad to provide guidance. As a token of gratitude for reading this book, I am providing a free one-on-one consultation to delve into your objectives and obstacles in any fintech sector covered in this book.

Just contact me via email at qamar.imran1@gmail.com and we can plan a time to get in touch. I am excited about the opportunity to assist you in achieving your goals and I am eager to help you turn your fintech vision into reality. Here's to embracing the opportunities, rising to the challenges, and shaping the future of finance together.